THE CAPITALISM DELUSION

Bob Ellis is the author of nineteen books, fifty-four screenplays, two hundred poems, five hundred political speeches and two thousand film reviews. His most recent work, *And So It Went: Night Thoughts in a Year of Change*, was also published in 2009. Previous titles include the bestselling *Goodbye Jerusalem*, *Goodbye Babylon* and *Night Thoughts in Time of War*. His 1998 book on economics, *First Abolish the Customer*, proves to have been impressively prophetic.

He co-wrote the classic films *Newsfront*, *Fatty Finn* and *Goodbye Paradise*. He is the co-author of the musical play *The Legend of King O'Malley*, the television miniseries *The True Believers* and the Ben Chifley play *A Local Man*. He wrote and directed the feature films *Unfinished Business* and *The Nostradamus Kid* and wrote and appeared in the documentary *Bastards from the Bush*, about his long friendship with the poet Les Murray. His work for film and stage has won numerous nominations and awards for writing and direction, including three Premier's Literary Awards, three AFIs, five AWGIES and a Critics' Circle Award.

His articles and essays in *HQ*, *Encore*, the *Age*, the *Sydney Morning Herald*, the *Canberra Times*, the *Courier-Mail*, *The Nation Review* and ABC website *Unleashed* have generated both enraged and enthusiastic responses. In 2002 he was voted Columnist of the Year by the Magazine Publishers Association.

He has had a long and close involvement with politics, covering as a journalist twenty-four campaigns in Australia, the UK and the US, and writing speeches for Kim Beazley, Bob Carr, Mike Rann, Nathan Rees and Kamahl. In 1994 he stood as an Independent against Bronwyn Bishop, who was then thought likely to lead the Liberal Party, and gained with her political puncturing a contentious, edgy, enduring national fame.

BOB ELLIS

THE CAPITALISM DELUSION

HOW GLOBAL ECONOMICS WRECKED EVERYTHING

AND WHAT TO DO ABOUT IT

A BOOK IN 345 ARGUMENTS

PENGUIN BOOKS

PENGUIN BOOKS

Published by the Penguin Group
Penguin Group (Australia)
250 Camberwell Road, Camberwell, Victoria 3124, Australia
(a division of Pearson Australia Group Pty Ltd)
Penguin Group (USA) Inc.
375 Hudson Street, New York, New York 10014, USA
Penguin Group (Canada)
90 Eglinton Avenue East, Suite 700, Toronto, Canada ON M4P 2Y3
(a division of Pearson Penguin Canada Inc.)
Penguin Books Ltd
80 Strand, London WC2R 0RL England
Penguin Ireland
25 St Stephen's Green, Dublin 2, Ireland
(a division of Penguin Books Ltd)
Penguin Books India Pvt Ltd
11 Community Centre, Panchsheel Park, New Delhi – 110 017, India
Penguin Group (NZ)
67 Apollo Drive, Rosedale, North Shore 0632, New Zealand
(a division of Pearson New Zealand Ltd)
Penguin Books (South Africa) (Pty) Ltd
24 Sturdee Avenue, Rosebank, Johannesburg 2196, South Africa

Penguin Books Ltd, Registered Offices: 80 Strand, London, WC2R 0RL, England

First published by Penguin Group (Australia), 2009

10 9 8 7 6 5 4 3 2 1

Cover and text design by Cameron Midson © Penguin Group (Australia)
Typeset in Monotype Dante by Post Pre-Press Group, Brisbane, Queensland
Printed and bound in Australia by McPherson's Printing Group, Maryborough, Victoria

National Library of Australia
Cataloguing-in-Publication data:

Ellis, Bob.

The capitalism delusion: how global economics wrecked
everything and what to do about it / Bob Ellis.

9780143203360 (pbk.)

Capitalism.
International economic relations.
Globalization.

337

penguin.com.au

To Alice Ellis,

my collaborator

ACKNOWLEDGEMENTS

The author wishes to thank, cum laude, Alice O'Keefe Ellis, who tirelessly excavated all the figures; Alex McDonald, her assistant; Michael Moore, auteur of *Sicko*; Naomi Klein, author of *Shock Doctrine: The Rise of Disaster Capitalism*; Peter Elkind and Bethany McClean, who co-wrote *Enron: The Smartest Guys in the Room*; Michael Lewis for his *Vanity Fair* piece on Iceland's bankrupting; Bob and Betty Con Walker, authors of *Privatisation: Sell Out Or Sell Off*; Winton Higgins, visiting research fellow at the Transforming Cultures Research Centre at UTS, who has vigilantly checked, now, both my books on economics; and John Maynard Lord Keynes, who knew it all sixty years ago and was lately proved right once again. My especial gratitude to Bob Sessions of Penguin who with buoyant vigour approved this book and its perilous deadline within an hour of its proposal, and its editors Katie Purvis and Michael Nolan who soothed it into its final form. And my wife Anne Brooksbank, its typist and guardian angel.

THINGS NOT SEEN

1

If I were to say to you, *Don't worry about the tsunami, the free market will sort it out,* you might think me a little mad.

Or if I were to say, *The Chinese earthquake? It isn't a problem.* The issues arising from a schoolhouse falling in and the one child of a one-child family being killed, and his father having had a vasectomy and his mother wanting another child to replace him, are issues that market forces will easily fix, you wait and see.

Or if I were to say to you, *The killing of three hundred children by Israeli bombardment? And the destruction of fifty thousand buildings? Don't worry.* The deregulated free market, unguided by government interference, will quickly fix all that.

Or the swamping of New Orleans, or the summer fires in Victoria, Australia, or the killing by machete of eight hundred thousand harmless Rwandans, are well within the power of the free market to sort out.

You would think me a little mad, or misguided, or

unapprised of the facts, would you not? You would wonder what planet I'd been living on.

You'd wonder if I was deluded.

2

Yet ideas pretty close to these have been espoused for twenty years by prizewinning economic thinkers, by heads of government, by influential journalists and university departments. The idea that government must be minimised, and market forces let rip, and all would be well.

I call it the Capitalism Delusion.

3

It was similar to the God Delusion – the idea that if you simply surrendered your heart to the Deity, his Invisible Hand would look after you through all the days of your life.

4

Or they didn't believe it, exactly. They touted it as a plausible philosophy, a working hypothesis they could live by, much as Christians believe that when you die it isn't the end of things, it's just a hushed and glimmering borderland you pass over on your way to a better world, a world in which there is a Level Playing Field, and this will sort things out.

It was less an economic theory than a faith-based religion and like another faith-based religion, Scientology – in which a lot of significant things happened on other planets before mankind came to this one – it believed in another reality, a world other than the one we are in.

In this world, the Capitalism Delusion asserts, there are no interrupting earthquakes, bushfires, wars, tornadoes, tribal pogroms, religious crusades, army coups, no summer blizzards nor hurricanes nor decomposing glaciers that alter the course of human life on earth and, with it, world economics.

There are no demigods like Elvis or Jesus or Shakespeare who attract a deluge of tourists to particular landmarks and cities.

There are no holy cities like Mecca or Disneyland whose millions of pilgrims alter the way their economies run.

There is indeed no remarkable exception (like, say, World War I, the Lisbon earthquake, the storms that smashed the Spanish Armada) to the orderly progress of the free market across the planet if that market is unleashed. For everyone will prosper then (albeit unequally) under its ever-spreading, ever-multiplying beneficence. All will be well.

This was their Faith, very like the one that Christians hold to, that everyone lives again, and in a beautiful crystal city enjoys himself immensely singing hymns among his relatives and ex-wives and drinking pure crystal water, abjuring alcohol and lying down with lions in perfect safety.

Faith, said St Paul, is the substance of things hoped for, the evidence of things not seen.

5

'Free market fundamentalism', as it is often called, held that money had no borders and like Empire it could overwhelm small nations, alter their cultures, reorder their agrarian economies into industrial, manufacturing ones, paying their subject peoples pittances, or what were then called 'slave wages', for goods (like Nike shoes) that then sold for an immense profit in the western world.

Being borderless, it interpenetrated economies ill-armed to resist its bad effects – urbanisation, pollution, foul slums, child prostitution, cigarettes, the opium trade – and its *worse* effects when the multinational company pulled out, and went to another country whose even more desperate wage slaves charged even less money for their services in factories and plantations.

Being borderless, and unconstrained by governments hungry for 'investment', it could write its own rules. It could smash, grab and move on. It had the ethic of the highway robber, and a good deal of the same sales pitch: *Your money or your life.*

6

Parallel to its rise, and what must now seem its golden age, was the rise of another borderless, interpenetrative, smash-grab-and-move-on way of thinking, which was Terrorism.

Wherever free market fundamentalism went and made buckets of money, Terrorism grew.

Like economic fundamentalism, it was nationless, it was conscienceless, it didn't mind busting up communities, scaring women, wrecking town centres, threatening ways of life. It had similar world-conquering goals and similar aggressive creativity.

7

Global free market fundamentalism, you might say, is the terrorism of money. And terrorism, stretching it a bit, the unfettered free market in competing means of death. Terrorism is international capitalism's furtive, stalking doppelganger; discuss.

Each has much to learn from the other, and the learning process continues. Capitalism knows now that a terrorist strike on a tunnel, a bridge, an airport, a sporting stadium, a Rolling Stones concert harms tourism, and commercial confidence, the national mood, and like an 'efficient' capitalist enterprise it is cheap, swift, targeted and, dare one say it, glamorous, since it has the glamour of heroic death.

Like fighter pilots in World War II.

8

It might be worthwhile to ask at this point, since the comparison has been made, why terrorism is so popular and why twenty million (perhaps) young men and women wouldn't mind, at this point, being a suicide bomber, and why a job in the financial services or hotel management does not much attract them.

Some would say it's because of the awful conditions international capitalism has brought to Muslim countries in Africa, the Middle East and the Subcontinent.

Some would blame Osama bin Laden, and the glamorous thrill he gave to his cause with the captured planes and the toppling towers of 9/11.

Some would blame the Islamic countries' senseless prohibition of drink, and their forbidding, moreover, of sex before marriage, which leaves male adolescents violently festering and keen to do mischief, gang-rape women, shoot infidels, blow up the world.

Some would blame it on Israel, and that bellicose country's neo-Biblical policy of 'a hundred eyes for an eye' which has killed at least one relative of every young male in the Middle East, and stirred him to thoughts of infernal revenge.

Revenge as well on Israel's principal sponsor, America, and America's proud discovery, international market fundamentalism, the theology, in Arab eyes, of 'the Great Satan' who must be brought down, like the Towers, in flames.

But the cause might not be any of these.

It might be Islam's traffic, for a thousand years, in what might be called 'the free market of ideas'.

9

Islam now has 1.3 billion fervent adherents, outnumbering fervent Catholics by (probably) three to one and fervent Protestants by four to one. Hinduism, at eight hundred and seventy-two million adherents, comes in a close second, and Buddhism fourth at a mere three hundred and eighty million. There may be more lurking Confucians in China than the one hundred million we know of, but they, once you add in fervour, must come in, at fifty-five million, a respectable fifth.

The question is, why has Islam attracted so many adherents? Its likely numbers by 2025 will be over two billion, an equivalent of the population of the earth in 1952. And its patriarchal ten-child families, or eight-child families, argue its popularity is on the increase.

Why *is* this? Why are there so many?

10

Well, in the free market of ideas, it offered the best deal. In the stock market of theologies, it appealed to the greatest number of likely customers.

What it offered was four wives, discardable at will, each of them selectable at age ten or twelve, whose infidelity,

Sharia law in some versions decreed, was punishable by death, by stoning to death.

Catholicism by contrast offered you an ever-ageing wife you could not get rid of, and must stop having sex with when she couldn't have children any more. For forty years, for eternity, you had to put up with her, and not lay a hand on her.

Okay then, customers: four young replaceable wives, anxious to please you (so they won't be replaced) on the one side, or the ever-ageing, stroppy and sex-free Aggie O'Farrell on the other. What are your bids for Aggie O'Farrell?

And thus it was that even though Islam offered no drink (except in the next life, where wine was paradoxically plentiful round the clock), it offered so much abundant sex (seventy-two eager virgins in the minute after a martyr's death, and if the martyr is a female she becomes the head virgin) that, *in the free market of ideas*, it had to prevail.

This leads us to wonder if markets indeed should be free, or if they should be regulated in some way that is to do with morality.

Whether market fundamentalism, in fact, is another way of saying moral chaos; discuss.

11

For, as a result of the international free market – the Invisible Hand that solves everything – one child dies every three seconds – from bad water, bad hygiene at birth, bad food or the high free-global-market cost of drugs that ward off inherited HIV in one's early years.

As a result of the international free global market, call it the IFGM, one million children are exploited in the sex industry every year, and 7.7 million under age five will die of communicable diseases, and six million suffer lives which the average US upper-middle-class citizen would not wish for his children. Lives involved with drug dealing, armed robbery, street begging, the killing with big paving stones of rival street beggars while they sleep.

Because of the international free market, tons of heroin, marijuana and cocaine pour over the Mexican border every month, and no policeman or politician who tries to stop it is safe from being murdered.

Free trade and murder, it seems, go hand in hand.

The alternative name for free trade, one might say, is 'licence to kill'; discuss.

12

Some say this killing would happen anyway, whatever sort of government or economic system we had, the smugglers would always get through. The children would always prostitute themselves. The bad water would always be bad. The junkies would always overdose.

But the history of one country refutes this. One country at least.

Its name is Cuba.

13

In the 1950s, Cuba benefited from what we would now call 'free market economics'. It had gambling casinos, jazz clubs, drugs and voluptuous young prostitutes. Its principal patrons, the Mafia, flew in rich celebrities for wild weekends.

Its waiters, barmen, drivers and girls-of-the-night were paid high fees and wages and the right-wing unions were very powerful. Drugs were plentiful and profitable to the free-market true believers who grew and sold them.

The children of peasant families in the hills, however, died a lot for want of a local doctor. Only forty percent of their children went to school, though many learned reading and math at home. The average per capita income was six dollars a week, compared to fifteen dollars ninety-four cents a week in Mississippi, the USA's poorest state. That six dollars a week would be fifty-four dollars a week today.

Fidel Castro and Che Guevara fought a war to overthrow Fulgencio Batista, the corrupt pro-American dictator. They came to power in January 1959, and Batista and his gangster associates fled.

By 1965 the literacy rate had risen from seventy-six percent to ninety-seven percent. Every peasant family had rapid access to a doctor. Every Cuban citizen had free education, including free university education. The casinos and brothels were closed. The rich landowners' property was redistributed to poor peasant share-farmers.

Twenty thousand pro-Batista activists were imprisoned, though, and tortured, and some executed, homosexuals were gaoled and 're-educated', Beatles music banned. Presidential elections, long promised, were never held, though local council elections were, and the nationalised restaurants were – and are – terrible.

Cuban doctors were soon famed for their skill and were sent all over the world, healing ailing peasants in Africa and, lately, East Timor. Fifteen hundred Cuban doctors were offered to America after Hurricane Katrina but President Bush refused them, the way he would.

Many disgruntled crooked businessmen fled Castro's regime and in Miami plotted his downfall. The Bay of Pigs followed, the Cuban Missile Crisis and twenty-six failed plots to assassinate Fidel with exploding cigars, poisoned wetsuits and a former mistress with lethal pills in a face-cream jar who found she liked him too much and, post-coitally, sobbing, did not follow through. He offered his gun and said, 'Shoot me', but she wouldn't. Six hundred and thirty-eight other plots were contemplated (we are told), but not enacted.

His regime outlasted ten US Presidents. His brother Raúl has restored a modicum of private enterprise and may, perhaps, come to a deal with Obama. This deal may end the embargo on all Cuban goods and all travel by US citizens to Cuba, whose vivacious music attracts them, and whose 'Calypso Communism' and uncorrupted leadership (Fidel and Raúl have no foreign bank accounts) seems different from the money-stashing Latin American norm.

After forty-seven years of embargo, stopping Americans going there, and land mines all around Guantanamo Bay so no banana vendors could sell their wares to gringos, it is said by economic experts and Fox News the Cuban economy has failed because of 'its own internal contradictions'.

It is hard to put a case for this.

14

You have to argue that seventy-six percent literacy is better economically than ninety-seven percent. That universal free health care (in hospitals admired worldwide) is worse economically than any alternative (like, say, the American system, *your money or your life*). That universal tertiary education is somehow a bad thing, bad for any economy. That free food and a free hotel room on your wedding night are bad things. That gambling casinos and child prostitution are good things.

You become, in short, involved, when you talk of these things, in questions of *economic morality*. You have to admit some living conditions, some social questions, outweigh the corporate bottom line. You have to say that market fundamentalism and humanist morality are at odds, or sometimes at odds; they sometimes go different ways.

And you have to choose which way you go – as an economist, as a politician, as a journalist, as a university tutor.

Rupert Murdoch would have killed Castro and restored Batista, and with him presumably the brothels, the Mafia and the gaming tables.

So would Bill O'Reilly, Sean Hannity, Charles Krauthammer, and many unnameable conservative Australian columnists.

How about you?

15

You could say I suppose that gigolos, prostitutes, fan dancers and croupiers don't need to be literate. Uninformed or not, unhappy or not, they serve the economy.

You could say that waiters, barmaids, hotel clerks and standover men don't need university degrees.

You could say an economy based on these people doesn't need an educated middle class of experimental scientists, history professors, brain surgeons, ballet dancers, hurricane salvage experts and so on.

You could say that free healthy food every day for everyone (no-one starves in Cuba) dulls the edge of husbandry.

But it's hard for you to say, or it should be hard for you to say, that a bottom-line-only economy that rejects the need for these ingredients of a civilisation, is a good economy.

It may deny the next Bill Gates or George Lucas an

education, and that's bad for the economy. It may deny the next Paul McCartney or Elvis Presley the food he needs (and the clean water he needs) to survive his infancy, and that's bad for the economy.

It may deny the next Stephen Hawking the medical care that preserves him to write his world-changing book, and that's bad for the economy.

Well, isn't it?

And it's *very* hard for you to say that the two hundred million South Americans who idolise Che Guevara have erred in their conclusions, and the several current South American rulers who redistribute land and share wealth like Fidel have no basis for their economic policies.

And you *can't* say, surely you *can't* say, as economic fundamentalists insist, that prostitution, disease, illiteracy, corruption, torture and ignorance are 'inevitable', that they happen whatever the economic system, that some people are *losers* whatever their rulers' politics, and that Jesus was right when he said, 'The poor you always have with you, but me not always', and it's better the system 'backs winners', helps the wealthy get more wealth and start moving it around.

No, no, no. The poor are the ones we *create* with our economic system.

The poor are the ones we trickle down on.

16

And you can't say either, you can't, I believe, in good con-
science any more say it would have been better for Cuba
if there had been forty-two thousand fewer doctors in the
last fifty years, and eighty-eight thousand more Cubans
dead in infancy from starvation, colic or bad water, and the
loss of John Lennon's music for twenty years, or that the
persecution of some homosexuals, and the rescue from
prostitution of some thirteen-year-old girls were too high a
price to pay, in sum, for these medical benefits to everyone.

Or can you?

How precisely do you do that?

17

Economic fundamentalism's core belief – that most
people are expendable and there is another kind of being,
a Superperson, whose needs come first, even though the
result of his needs is the suffering and death of others – is
a belief we should probably now examine.

The Superperson is a shareholder, and in his interests
the system fires, retrenches, asset-strips and moves offshore industrial entities that have been the core and vitality
of towns and small cities and ways of life, *and no editorial-
ist says this is wrong*, that a worker who has for twenty-five
or forty years helped make the goods that built up the
company's wealth has at least as many rights as the lately
interloping rich man who, on his accountant's advice,

has bought some shares in a company that might now be moving overseas.

Somehow this rich man is someone a worker should sacrifice his life for, and somehow the CEO who sacked him and three thousand others one afternoon deserves an eight-million-dollar bonus (the equivalent of five hundred factory workers' annual wages) for doing so.

All men are equal, it seems, but the Shareholder is much more equal that others. He is a Superperson and you must bow down to his needs, his needs for a yacht and a villa in Tuscany and two pampered ex-wives.

They outweigh yours.

It stands to reason.

You have to look at the Big Picture.

18

The Big Picture suggests that the 2.3 million US citizens now in gaol and (at an educated guess) the thirty million US citizens now alive who have been in gaol, and the thirty thousand US citizens killed by gunfire every year, and the two hundred and thirty-three thousand women raped every year in that country, and the forty-two million living in 'working poverty' in that country, and the forty-eight million without adequate health care, are the necessary casualties, the expendable exceptions to American happiness, the collateral damage of an excellent system that is currently working as well as a system can, a system that needs only a bit more *dereg-ulation* to work very well indeed, to be the best kind of system there is.

The system whose Invisible Hand will look after us.

19

I disagree with this.

The system *won't* look after you when the chips are down. This is evidenced by what happened on the upper floors of AIG in mid-2008.

The company insured other companies for toxic loans that, in an economic downturn, lost one hundred and seventy billion dollars and this debt was paid by the Bush government because AIG was 'too big to fail' and would cause a world depression, it was said, if it was not rescued.

The AIG executives then paid themselves one hundred and sixty-five million dollars in bonuses *for good work* although they had nearly, in the previous year, sent the whole world broke. Some of the bonuses were three million dollars, some only a million, some as little as five hundred and fifty thousand dollars.

But they would, in total, have sustained for a year on their usual earnings two thousand lesser AIG employees.

Spending the money on employees' wages would also not have brought AIG into ridicule and contempt world-wide, and reduced its share value in a wave of worldwide arithmetical revulsion.

20

Four hundred and sixty-three executives were involved in this legal swindle.

They were not 'a few bad apples'.

They were a typical cross-section, an unexceptional sample, of people involved in the financial services business, the economic sector.

Which proves (or am I wrong?) that economic fundamentalists do not *care* what happens to society or western civilisation or the world at large, or even their own workmates, or their own shareholders, just so long as they get, as payout, enough to live on in prosperous comfort for the rest of their lives.

This is a very telling fact, and a lot of people picked up on it and grew very angry, and subsequent public demonstrations threatened the job of Obama's Treasury Secretary, Tim Geithner, for having let it happen.

The very core of capitalism itself, the urge to personal profit, the throbbing impulse of personal greed, came into disrepute. A lot of people thought capitalism 'had gone too far' and leashes and muzzles and handcuffs and shackles should be put on it thereafter.

Down, boy, down, the people said.

21

This was because, I think, I suggest, I warily suggest, most people weren't very fond of capitalism in the first place.

They didn't like its risks and humiliations.

They didn't like its unequal rewards.

No-one was prepared to fight and die for it, the way Che was for Hispanic Socialism.

They might fight and die for freedom of speech, they might fight and die to save Europe's Jews from the Holocaust, but not to preserve the real-estate billions of Donald Trump or the media billions of Rupert Murdoch, or the millions paid to Tom Cruise for grinning cheekily, or the millions Bill O'Reilly gets each year for bullying, bluster and bare-faced lies.

They didn't like the idea of leaping through successive hoops of fire for twenty years to achieve your first million.

Or the dodgy or criminal means by which you thereafter made your pile.

They didn't like the criminals who did well out of the system, like Alan Bond and Christopher Skase and Jeff Skilling and Bernard Madoff.

They wondered how many other criminals were still doing well out of it, undiscovered.

They weren't that keen on capitalism in the first place.

So when AIG revealed itself as a bunch of greedy, cheating shysters they began to wonder if capitalism should be replaced.

Replaced by something nicer.

What would that be?

22

It's worth noting that nicer systems have been tried, some of them pretty successfully.

In Sweden in the 1970s, for instance, the wages of a CEO were as a rule no more than four times what his company's lowliest worker got, the janitor or whoever, unemployment benefits were ninety percent of your previous wage, old-age pensions were two thirds of your previous wage, and hospitals, schools and universities were free. Few people owned cars or houses with lawns but the trains and trams went everywhere, the cafes were cheap, the lifestyle promiscuous and, in the cities, uncensorious and the civilisation so good that only two hundred and ten native Swedes migrated in any year, most of them to other parts of Scandinavia, where conditions were similar.

23

The system was called Social Democracy and it held that the need of the many was more important than the greed of the few. It was paid for by a fifty percent tax and the earnings of union-participant industries, in particular Volvo and Saab, whose exquisite automobiles were well-made, glamorous, safe and sold everywhere.

Swedes believed a fifty percent tax was a reasonable price for lifelong health, education and security. They travelled through Europe in their holidays, had fine subsidised theatre lifelong and excellent subsidised cinema – Ingmar

Bergman, Vilgot Sjöman, Kay Pollak – had no money worries in their old age, an average life span of eighty, and yes, committed suicide sometimes but only as much as the world average.

Some said they committed suicide because their lives were so dull and sheltered, so subsidised, predictable and full of empty sex. Others said it was because their doctors were honest and labelled as suicide what other cultures' doctors covered up, and their suicide rate in fact was normal, and a lot of it what we would now call consensual euthanasia.

Why isn't this way of living tried in other countries, you may ask?

Well, it is actually, with variants. In Denmark, Norway, Finland, Greenland, Holland, Austria, West Germany, Nicaragua, Brazil, Argentina, Venezuela and Bolivia variants on this system are, with caveats, still in play.

But you would never know.

In the English-speaking countries we look to America for example.

And see what happened there.

24

In September, October, November and December of 2008 one-third of America's money vanished.

Though George Bush with seven hundred billion paid out the corporate incompetents' debts, eighty thousand jobs were lost in a month. Loans were called in, house prices crashed and one house in Michigan was sold for a dollar (to a man who beat the vendor down, the joke goes, from a dollar eighty-five). Houses vacated by families who thereafter lived in their cars or on the grimy garage floors of relatives were looted and smashed by unbenevolent neighbours and the sackings continued, and so did a war in Iraq that was costing eight billion dollars a month.

That eight billion dollars could have kept two hundred thousand workers in useful employment for a year. And five months of the war would have kept a million workers in useful employment for a year. A year of the war, 2.4 million workers, and so on.

But these were not thought by economic fundamentalism, by the Capitalism Delusion, to be useful people. Far better that money was spent on the bonuses of two hundred incompetent financial managers who were rich already, and on bombs and rockets given to Israel cost-free that blew up children and provoked a further thousand years of fratricidal, tribal and civil wars, than on harmless honest workers trying to raise children and pay a mortgage.

And the Invisible Hand said, 'So be it. This is the light in our day. This is the way the world must be henceforth and forever.

'There is no alternative.'

25

At the heart of the Capitalism Delusion is the fixed belief that a CEO of a big corporation is worth his hire, and worth his day's pay (of, on average, forty thousand dollars *per day*) and he does useful work.

It is often hard to see what that useful work is.

Max Moore-Wilton, for instance, ran the Sydney Airport Corporation for three years and was paid thirty-two dollars a minute (day and night, waking and sleeping) for doing so and was given five million dollars for going away. The interest he gets, if he wants it, on this five million will be six hundred and eighty-five dollars *a day* for the rest of his life.

His job was to make sure planes landed, passengers came safely through Customs and sufficient taxis, hire cars, trains and buses took them away.

These things happened the way they always had, with underlings making sure they happened, and his tenure as CEO didn't make a blind bit of difference to this unaltered, routine reality.

Recently, in fact, to prove this, a bikie bashed another bikie's head in and killed him in the check-in area and Max's successor Russell Balding said it wasn't his or Max's fault. Though customer safety was one of the things he was responsible for, it was a police matter, he said. And clearly he or Max Moore-Wilton hadn't provided for this possibility.

There are arguments, reader, to say that the workings of Sydney Airport would have been no different if Max Moore-Wilton and Russell Balding had never been born.

And yet they got thirty-two dollars a minute, day and night, seven days a week, for being airport CEO.

Why?

Discuss.

26

David Owens, head of Thames Water, is like this. He makes sure water comes clean out of taps, though he's never repaired one, and gets paid ninety-four pounds an hour every day of the year, twenty-four hours of the day, just for being there and being called CEO.

There are people all over the world like this, heading road construction companies and hamburger-delivering entities, whose effective duties could be done by a moron working two hours a year, and yet they get millions of dollars just to be there, just for being CEO.

Why?

It's probably a memory of the Divine Right of Kings.

The king didn't have to be useful, just *be*. He was a God-ordained fact, and you had to reverence and worship him. He was a deity, deserving of massive congratulation, just for being there.

27

And some of them are even worse than that. They bring poison to the system.

Some of them do.

When the world's safest airline, Qantas, was privatised, for instance, a series of CEOs who ran it sacked people who apparently weren't needed any more.

They sacked stewardesses and luggage handlers and ticket salesmen and booking agents all over the world.

They 'downsized' big numbers of engineers they needed to fix the planes' engines, the way you do.

Under Geoff Dixon, the CEO from 2001 to 2008, five thousand Qantas workers were retrenched.

Then Qantas started to fall out of the sky.

28

On July 25th, 2008, flight QF3 was interrupted when a luggage compartment blew out and the plane fell twenty thousand feet, ears popped and baggage was sucked out. Oxygen masks were used and a number of passengers applauded when the diverted plane landed in Manila and some of them vomited on the tarmac. There was a nine-foot hole in the fuselage. 'It was a like a tyre exploding,' said a passenger, 'but more violently.'

On October 7th, 2008, flight QF72 from Singapore was nearing Perth when it had an 'unexpected altitude change', several passengers hit the roof and thirty-six people were injured, twenty severely. The air-bus executed an emergency landing in Learmonth and the Flying Doctor Service took thirteen of the more severely tossed-about to Perth. Though this 'significant safety event' (SSE) was found to be a rogue atmospheric accident and not Qantas's fault, much damage had been done, and minor incidents thereafter (long waits for luggage, late arrivals, delayed takeoffs) were magnified in the headlines.

Geoff Dixon got 5.54 million dollars in wages and bonuses that year (or the equivalent wages of one hundred and eighty-four of the thousands of Qantas workers he sacked to pay for himself and his own special needs, the yacht, the villa and so on) and, as a bonus, twelve million dollars more as he was leaving.

He got forty-two million dollars in all while Qantas's reputation for safety eroded and people's lives were endangered, or presumably endangered; discuss.

The interest on this sum, should he care to receive it, is five thousand four hundred and fifty-three dollars *a day* for the rest of his life.

Discuss.

29

Though it's hard to know what some CEOs do, there is one thing all of them do.

They sack people. They sack loyal workers who have

been in the company, building its wealth and good name, for twenty, thirty years and thus impose the bottom line.

They don't sack them face to face of course. That would be too much like hard work. They get some other poor underling, doped on Xanax, to do that for them.

They often don't even draw up a list.

They merely say to their number two: 'Take forty-two old-timers out of the Sydney office. Offer them handsome redundancies. And then, a day later, *less* handsome redundancies.'

For this they get paid millions a year.

Global capitalism is about sacking people; discuss.

Let the planes crash or the striking baggage handlers beweep their new exhaustion and the passengers wait an extra hour for their things.

The sackings must go on.

The economy demands it.

30

Does an economy serve the people, or do the people serve the economy?

And who is 'the economy'?

Just asking.

31

It's the shareholders, it seems, the Superpersons, and the yawning Board and the dronelike CEOs. It's for their extra money that jobs go overseas and lives are distorted, mar-riages endangered, wives beaten, alcoholics rehabilitated, grief counsellors underpaid.

The shareholders and the CEOs like the money.

And, according to economic fundamentalism, they deserve it.

They have to deserve it.

For capitalism makes no sense, no sense at all, if they don't deserve it.

They deserve the millions each we pay them, or capital-ism makes no sense.

THE VARYING PRICE
OF A ROOF

32

In September, October, November and December 2008 forty percent of the world's money vanished.

Where did it go? Can we print some more? Why not?

The reason, we're told, is that it never existed, or truly existed, in the first place.

It was only the value put on property, or on the debt accruing to that property, which the various banks and corporations had or, for the moment, had controlled.

Debts for houses bought when interest rates were one percent and could no longer be paid when interest rates went up to five percent were thought to be worth, in money, the price – or the initial price in 2003 – of that house.

But as factories closed and jobs went offshore – as economic fundamentalism, you might say, kicked in – workers in hock for the price of their houses could no longer afford them, even at one percent.

And the houses in thousands went on the market and the prices plummeted.

And the value of loans held by banks that were passed on to hedge funds went down, way down, grew 'toxic', and the assumed wealth vanished.

And because each debt propped up, like a vertebra, some part of the long rickety spine of global finance, it soon fell down into a shambles – the international shambles that we now call 'The Great Recession'.

This leads us to ask the core and fundamental question:

Why is there such variation in the cost of a dwelling? Why, in short, does the price of a roof so vary?

A roof is a human addiction. It keeps out the rain. Like certain drugs (heroin, tea, hot chocolate, beer, Xanax) it gives us a sense of calm. It prevents old people from getting pneumonia and children being scared at night by sinister shapes in the trees.

A roof is a popular emollient. But what, as a rule, does it cost?

33

There is no rule to this, it seems.

A budget motel in Wagga Wagga costs forty-five dollars a night. A hotel in New York costs four thousand five hundred dollars a night. A hostel bed in Devonport, Tasmania, twenty-two dollars a night. A stateroom on the *Queen Mary 2* a thousand dollars a night.

The customer in each case is protected from being rained on, warm in bed, with access to a colour television, but he is charged inordinately for those extra things – a conference room, a minibar, a swirl-bath, an ocean view – that he doesn't strictly need.

He is charged, in fact, in thousands a night, for a feeling he gets of status. Of being approved, acclaimed by the surroundings in which, for a night or the length of an ocean cruise, he is monarch of all he surveys.

34

The same thing is true for him when he comes to buy a house.

He can buy in Eritrea a half-acre compound of rickety chook-houses capable of accommodating in rude comfort an eighteen-member extended family, four dogs and twenty hens for eight thousand five hundred dollars.

Or he can buy a one-bedroom flat in Tokyo with a city view and a swirl-bath for *two million* dollars. This might accommodate in fair comfort two people and exclude any animals whatever.

And it costs two hundred and thirty-five times as much as the Eritrea compound.

Why the discrepancy?

The Eritrea compound has many advantages. It has built-in babysitters and playmates for its many children. It has room to keep chickens in and a courtyard barbecue table for family gatherings. It has a feeling of mutual support and family affection, and though squabbles break out and occasional acts of marital violence, it has a unanimity of purpose and a group-hug loyalty that will leave the children largely untraumatised and ready to face the world.

Whereas in the Tokyo flat there may be no children at all.

There will be the occasional shared swirl-bath and nights at home watching TV and eating takeaway sashimi but no great immersion in human life, as we understand it, or as we want to understand it, at all.

35

How does this discrepancy in house prices, and consequent ways of life, occur? How can the free market, when it comes to the price of dwellings, be said to be wise, and price regulation (as happens in command economies) be said to be just plain wrong?

36

In County Galway the average price of a stone cottage went up from nine thousand punts, or Irish pounds, in 1974 to three hundred thousand punts in 2009.

This meant anyone buying it at the latter price would have to give up a good deal of his or her life to service the mortgage.

In contrast to 1979, he or she could no longer afford a weekend cruise to the Aran Islands, many restaurant meals or nights over Guinness pie at the pub or fresh cuts of meat to cook at home or tango lessons at the church priory.

To afford his stone hovel and patch of ground, a romantic dream he has had since boyhood, he has to give up most of his lifestyle.

If the interest rates go up, as they will tend to do, he (or she) has to give up even more. One more restaurant meal. The trip he planned to take to Venice with a girlfriend.

How did this all happen? How did the fates conspire to cost him so much happiness? How is he made by mere economics to sacrifice so much for the house of his dreams?

How is it likely that in contrast to the peasant owners of that property two generations back, who could somehow afford twelve children, he can afford only one?

37

Why has the price of a house, a flat, gone up so much?

You can still buy a second-hand caravan for five thousand dollars, which sometimes, depending on where you park it, has a water view. Why does a flat with similar amenities – two beds, a kitchen table, a toilet, a shower, a stove, a fridge and handy access to quality shops – cost a hundred times as much? Why is a dwelling on wheels so reprehensible, and a dwelling perched on fifty other dwellings in a drug-pushing, polluted neighbourhood so much better an idea?

38

A similar question arose in the author's family regarding the seaside block my father Keith bought in 1946 in Fingal, an unfashionable backwater in coastal New South Wales, on a sandy half-acre of land between a slimy lagoon and a pristine beach, for five pounds. With friends' help he built on it, in concrete bricks manufactured on the spot, a rudimentary two-room dwelling we would go to at Christmas.

My sister Kay eventually inherited it, and built above and around it, spending a hundred thousand dollars, a beautiful, spacious dwelling she, her husband, daughter, son-in-law and grandsons now live in.

The property is now worth 1.1 million dollars. Eight hundred thousand of the value is the land. It has water on either side.

No assessment of inflation in the Australian economy can account for the rise in land value by eighty *thousand* percent.

If the land value had gone up at the same rate as the average wage, it would now cost one thousand one hundred and two dollars. And it currently costs, if Kay cares to sell it and some poor fool to buy it, seven hundred and twenty-six times that amount.

How did this occur?

39

The economic fundamentalists would have us believe it happens naturally.

As the population increases, they assert, and the number of seaside blocks does not increase, *the natural workings of the market force up the value of my dad's five-pound purchase to eight hundred thousand dollars.* And if the poor fool has to spend forty-two percent of his household income paying it off, well, tough on him. The Invisible Hand has decided things should be this way, and There Is No Alternative, TINA, as Mrs Thatcher used to say.

(We'll come to her in a minute.)

This *is* what they say, these level-playing-field apostles of the Economic Inevitable, the way things have to be.

But is it in fact the case?

Does it really happen this way?

It did, surely, didn't it?

40

No, actually.

I am told by secret informants that this is wrong. I am told that if you believe this fancy Mendelian hypothesis you have fallen into error.

Australia has a small population and one of the longest coastlines of any country in the world. Beachfront properties, and water-view properties, should not be, as they are, as expensive as luxury apartments overlooking Central

Park in trendier, more populous and crowded New York. Why do they cost as much in a country so sparsely populated with so much land to acquire and develop and so many water views?

What actually happens (I am told) is this.

41

A bank buys four houses in the same street for a hundred and twenty-five thousand dollars each.

A year later, it sells one of them, by prearrangement, to another part of the bank, or an affiliated bank or financial entity, for a hundred and eighty thousand dollars.

Six months later this entity sells it back to the bank for two hundred and forty thousand dollars.

A year later the bank puts it on the market for three hundred and ten thousand dollars and *lends money at eight percent* to the poor fool who buys it.

He feels he has to buy it because the prices are currently going up so fast. He has to get in now, or he will never get in.

The bank then sells the other three properties in the same street, having rented them out in the meantime, to three other fools for three hundred and twenty-five thousand dollars each, a mark-up of two hundred thousand dollars, or one hundred and sixty percent, in two and a half years.

And, seeing what people are paying for indifferent

inner-suburban or beach-suburb houses with tiny lawns, the real estate agents begin to put similar prices on similar clapped-out wood-and-fibro dwellings, and the prices inexorably rise.

And the banks lend money at eight percent, and in some years seventeen percent, to the fools who buy them at that price.

And the real estate agents pocket up to four percent, that is twenty-five thousand dollars or so, of each new high price.

42

The result has been a social catastrophe.

The average working Australian does not spend any more, as he did in the 1950s, twenty-four percent of his disposable wage on his mortgage, but one hundred and twenty percent. His wife works too in at least a part-time job to make ends meet and because of the financial pressure she delays having children until her early or middle thirties – or her late thirties or early forties – and has, on average, only 1.93 of them, where her grandmother in 1961 had 3.5. She has at least one miscarriage and neglects the one or two children that have survived because she is working, and is in no fit state to gratify her exhausted husband when he comes home after working late in a job he detests and goes drinking, and sometimes skirt-chasing, because of.

He so exhausts himself in his prime years, his thirties

and forties, shovelling banknotes into the furnace of his mortgage and shouting at his wife and avoiding his children and chasing muff, that in time, pretty often, a divorce results, and the house he gave up so much for is sold, and in two grimy flats in less appealing suburbs, he, his wife and his traumatised and divided children (already smoking tobacco and drinking vodka and keen to try worse drugs) regard the ashes of their marriage, their grand illusion, with discontentment, find other partners, have or adopt other children, have side affairs and take on other mortgages on other worse houses that *still cost too much.*

43

If their first house (a Coogee hovel with a sliver of water view) had cost not seven hundred and eighty thousand but *one* hundred and eighty thousand, their lives would have been different.

She would not have had to work in her prime, child-bearing years. They could have afforded more children. The children, with siblings and an available consoling mother, would have grown up less alone. They would not have had to move to another suburb, losing their peer group, after the divorce. They would not now be, as some of them are, on crack cocaine.

The economy, moreover, would be the better for it. More money, much more money, would have been spent on soap and soup and shoes and schoolbooks, on cinema tickets and elective dental crowns and lean meat and fresh fruit and family vacations in caravan parks and seaside hotels and memorable rides on luxury trains and ski holidays.

The economy would have been booming, as it was in the 1950s, when a one-job couple spent only twenty-four percent of their household income on a mortgage, or eleven percent on house rental.

There was more spending money around in those days. And it was spent, in the human way, on pleasurable things.

44

It isn't now, because houses and rents cost too much. An average house in Melbourne required in 2008 an average mortgage payment, over twenty-five years, *of seven hundred and eighty percent of an average wage.*

This is the central fact of the western economies and nobody till August 2008 (when house prices dropped to a dollar in Michigan) did anything about it.

45

This was when some leading, respected economists discovered, surprise, surprise, that a man who can afford to buy a one–hundred-and-forty-thousand-dollar house in Michigan when he has a job, at an interest rate of one percent, cannot keep up payments on that house when he loses that job and the interest rates go up to four and five percent.

When the amount he has to pay each week quadruples.

A year ago I wrote in a column that is widely read that house prices that were three and four times what they ought to be were 'the elephant in the room', and if they kept rising, and if the interest rates kept rising, 'then everything would go to hell'.

46

And so it has come to pass.

And we have to begin to decide, as if starting from scratch, what is, and what should be, the variable cost of a roof.

And what a fair rent should be.

And whether it is fair that a couple who can only afford a one-bedroom flat in a grimy suburb should in fear and longing and solemn yearning decide they can't afford to have any children at all.

There are millions of worthy, intelligent people *not being born* because of economic fundamentalism; discuss.

But . . . there is no alternative.

Even though the 1950s worked quite well, with fewer divorces, drug busts, alcoholics, murders, fatal car crashes, teenage mothers, drug-addled prostitutes, hit men, gang wars, enslaved illegal immigrants and the rest of it.

47

'There is no alternative' (TINA) is what Mrs Thatcher used to say.

The woman who with some harsh, emphatic, half-cocked simplicities caused the greedy eighties and the innumerate lunacies of Ronald Reagan, and thereby wrecked the world.

Her husband was an oil executive who subsidised with millions that she never earned (nor he either, really) her brilliant career.

He called her 'the boss' and she was very bossy.

She told the non-millionaires of England they were 'moaning Minnies' who should 'get on their bike' when they lost their job and find another.

She closed the coal mines down when she didn't have to, destroying many working-class lives, the way she liked to, turning young men into street beggars living in cardboard boxes with their pit bull terriers in the Strand, and was told by Ronald Reagan and other economic fundamentalists that she had 'balls' and was 'the toughest man in England', because she didn't mind wrecking lives in her hot pursuit of the bottom line.

The number of suicides she caused is unknown but would be in the tens of thousands.

Think about that for a while.

There *was* an alternative, that these dry bones might live, and she chose that they would die.

What a cruel, crazy bitch she is.

(More of her later.)

48

Summing up thus far.

We have seen, thus far, that CEOs' wages and house prices are far too high and share-price hikes far too cruelly achieved and these three things bring such evil in their train that all the western economies are now in danger, and *in part* because of them, because of these things in part, capitalism is becoming seen by many thinking observers, and many ordinary people, to have failed.

To have been a delusion, a snare and a delusion.

This book will show they are not the only causes of why it has failed, if it ever in fact was tried, which the author will argue it was not, but they are some of them.

49

So what do we do?

There is no particular difficulty in limiting by legislation what CEOs get for their incompetent sloth, limiting it, say, to four times the wage of the President of the United States, and making them give back their bonuses when they stuff the company up.

But what else do we do?

About house prices, the early-onset diabetes of the economy of the world?

. . . No, no, not yet.

More of this later.

Till then let us look at a few more delusions.

THERE IS NO ALTERNATIVE

50

There is no alternative, economic fundamentalism said, to the privatisation of the means of production, distribution and exchange.

Government should get out of the way, and let private enterprise do what government does, or *most* of what government does, more efficiently.

'More efficiently' means it sacks more people, 'downsizing' its worldwide operation to the bare bones of its minimum.

51

In privatised prisons, for instance, a minimum number of big, brutal guards, former soldiers, bikies, thugs or Tongan sportsmen willing to travel 'settle rioting prisoners down'.

They don't let the prisoners out of their cells much and what, in pairs, they do inside them is their own private (privatised) affair.

Prisoners, moreover, are paid 'minimum wages', what

we would call slave wages, to clean the toilets, wash the dishes and make things – like folding tables, upholstered chairs and work benches – which the privatised entity then sells outside the prison for a profit.

In Woomera Detention Centre, where people caught trying to enter Australia – Hazaras fleeing the Taliban in fear of decapitation, Shi-ite Iraqis fleeing Saddam in fear of torture in Abu Ghraib, Palestinians fleeing Gaza in fear of 'targeted assassination' – were kept for three or five years before being (sometimes) sent home to their worst nightmares and death, prisoners (they were also called 'detainees') were allowed to do useful work for fifty-three cents an hour and, with the money earned, buy a phone card and with it speak to a relative, priest or solicitor for three minutes.

They would work for fifteen hours for the privilege of that short, frantic phone call, and be overcharged for it.

And, if they survived their repatriation and wished to try again to enter Australia in a more merciful era, they were then obliged to pay back one hundred and fifty dollars a day for it, a total of one million dollars for one family I know, for their previous 'luxury accommodation' in the privatised prison, a grim affair with razor wire, beatings, attempted suicides, sewn lips and the smashed toys of scared children.

It was in this way shown that the private administration of a government entity was a good idea, because it was run more 'efficiently', that is, more cheaply, by a multi-national business less concerned than government would have been with minor details like the Geneva Conventions and human rights.

Like other privatised concerns doing government business (like Blackwater, for instance, the 'private security firm' that in the streets of Baghdad was for eight years licensed to kill), this firm, whose name was Australasian Correctional Management or ACM, was licensed to torture.

But they ran the prison (or 'facility') more cheaply, that was the main thing. They saved their principal client, the Howard government, money.

And that had to be good for everyone.

52

With a like-minded motive, John Major proposed to privatise the railways of Britain.

He was thrown out before he could complete this.

But his conqueror, Tony Blair, did not fulfil his party's earlier commitment to keep the railways in the public sector. Instead, he left the new structure in place, and enigmatically completed the selling-off of what remained of the revered British institution to private enterprise.

It was broken up into twenty-nine entities, Northern Rail, London Midland, Arriva Trains Wales, Merseyrail,

Chiltern Railways, Heathrow Express, Gatwick Express, East Midlands Trains and so on, and nine thousand eight hundred railway workshop employees sacked because they were now unnecessary.

The survivors had to compete with each other as more jobs were made redundant, and with other privatised rail companies whose CEOs sought their customers.

(There were, of course, now twenty-nine train-operating-company CEOs instead of one Transport Minister, Glenda Jackson, the former film star, seen frequently nude in Ken Russell films, and a bureaucrat.)

The tragic farce that followed was dramatised in Ken Loach's film *The Navigators*, in which friends became enemies and an underprotected workman was killed by an uncoupled carriage.

The great train disaster of Ladbroke Grove in 1999, in which thirty-one passengers died and more than five hundred were injured, and a rise in rail fares of sometimes seventy percent, put paid to the noble experiment of railway privatisation.

It wasn't more efficient after all.

It cost much more.

And it killed people.

And destroyed, by sackings, many human lives.

The government had to 'renationalise' various incompetent rail entities, at a cost that was thought disastrous.

Like Tony Blair's other bright idea, the Iraq war, it did

no Englishman or Scotsman or Welshman or Northern Irishman any good at all.

A few CEOs perhaps, who made a bag of money and tiptoed away.

53

Similar privatisations – of Qantas, which started falling out of the sky, of Sydney Airport, now judged 'the worst in Australia', of South Australian electricity, 'leased' in a bizarre experiment for two hundred years by the *Chinese government*, now undergoing outages and blackouts that cause old people to die in sweltering houses in summer, and charging a hundred and twenty-five percent of what it used to in electricity bills (and a hundred and ninety percent to large industrial concerns) – have been comparably foolish and disappointing.

As usual, the customers pay more now than they did to the government to these 'more efficient' concerns.

It is wondered why it is done at all.

54

Corruption is frequently, though not always, part of it.

Putin sold off to his criminal confederates and KGB co-workers vast mining, electricity and defence-contract entities worth hundreds of billions for very low prices, and ordered the murder of journalists and broadcasters who complained about this old-boy network.

Bush after waging war in Iraq tried privatising its oil wealth so it could be sold off for pittances to crony companies Exxon and BP, but the Iraqi politicians wouldn't let him do it.

And all over the western world, any scrutiny will show, Cabinet ministers in charge of the entity sold off tend to join its Board of Directors a couple of years later, after prematurely leaving politics, and then get annual fees of half a million dollars for attending a couple of meetings.

All privatisations tend to corrupt (as the adage has it), but privatisations after 1990 tend to corrupt absolutely.

55

Why privatise anything?

It's a fair question.

The confident answer from economic fundamentalism is that government has no business in anything that private enterprise, cutting costs, could run for a profit.

Let government handle the *big* things, they say, like war, flood, cyclones, earthquakes and terrorist nuclear attack, while we in private enterprise handle the lesser things, like electricity, transport, cancer hospitals, AIDS drugs, universities, postal services and big aeroplanes. Besides, there's money in them, and we need and like money. The government doesn't need money, we do.

The reasonable answer to this is if the government can be trusted with the big things, like war and earthquake, flood and pestilence, why can't they be trusted with lesser things like postal delivery and telephone calls?

Why would it be wrong to keep doing what they've been praised for doing – British Rail, Qantas, Telstra – for decades, centuries, epochs?

How does it follow that someone unskilled in it, some corporate accountant, would do it better?

And has he in fact done it better?

What privatisation has worked?

Do you know of any?

Me neither. Across the world the track record is pretty grim.

56

Telstra, for instance, was privatised in stages by the Howard government, shares in it sold to 'Australian mums and dads' for around three dollars each, and a Mexican–American, Sol Trujillo, put in charge of it.

Telstra is, was, the Australian phone service. For sixty years it had put up phone lines, installed phones and repaired them, installed and repaired public phones, charged different fees for different hours and, lately, got room on a satellite for mobile phone calls.

Nobody much had complained about Telstra and almost nobody wanted it privatised.

But here Sol Trujillo was, being paid an average of eleven million a year to 'sort it out', as if it was in trouble, which it wasn't, and he brought with him three further gringos, known as 'the three amigos' to assist him in this mighty task, this monstrous crisis he saw looming.

He sacked ten thousand employees, telephone linesmen, repairmen and the like. He tore telephone boxes out of the shopping centres of country towns. It was too expensive to have that many, he said, and people sometimes stole money from them.

He made most of the remaining public phones accessible only by special cards available at newsagents, which were closed at night when many emergency calls – midwives needed, overdoses progressing, old people having seizures – occurred.

People died from Sol (privatising essential services is a licence to kill; discuss) and a hundred and twenty, maybe, or maybe only four, of the many he sacked committed suicide for want of a better alternative. And maybe they didn't. They certainly endured lesser lives.

The loss of the jobs and of the repairmen devastated several country towns and families moved out of them to city fringes looking for jobs.

The sacked men had done nothing wrong, but Sol, on eleven million a year, felt he needed to remove them or he'd be accused of not *doing* anything.

Of not being necessary, which he wasn't.

57

He did some things in collusion with foreign entities which the Howard government objected to and then forbade because they further endangered Australian jobs, and he became incensed, and plotted to bring down the Howard government, to whom he owed everything, because he wasn't getting freedom enough.

Relations between government and privatised entity worsened. They quarrelled in the headlines.

During Sol's reign the Telstra share price fell from five dollars to three dollars twenty-one.

The price of local phone calls went up.

The rival telco, Optus, was charged a fortune for using Telstra lines.

Sol announced his retirement in 2008, and walked away with thirty-one million dollars, plus a swag of diminished shares. He then called Australians 'racists' for mocking in cartoons his Mexican heritage.

Thirty-one million dollars would fund five small theatre companies for a thousand years on the interest alone.

Or pay eighty linesmen or repairmen their wages for ten years.

58

But Sol deserved the pay he got for what he did, bringing down the value of Telstra shares and devastating many small mum-and-dad investors and their plans for their old-age seaside retirements and raising the price of a phone call by, oh, twenty percent and ripping public phones out of country towns, or so the story goes. And so did the three amigos, who scuttled severally away, one of them, Greg Winn, with a total of twenty-one million more – or the cost of fifty more linesmen for ten years. (Or two small theatre companies for a thousand years on the interest alone.)

But nobody, strangely, counts *this* privatisation a success.

People can't see why it was *necessary*.

And, with privatisations, nobody ever can.

59

Why privatise anything?

What is the *argument* for privatising anything?

Certain rich people make a great wad of money from it, that's all.

60

Blackwater, for instance, is a privatised army.

They more efficiently guard, kidnap and kill people (it is said) than regular army, who are less well paid.

A Blackwater man gets around twelve hundred dollars a day, in contrast with a normal grunt, who gets one hundred and ninety dollars a day.

The owner Erik Prince has been paid one billion since

2001 to run Blackwater (and change its name from time to time), though what he does is hard to imagine.

Draws names out of a hat, I guess.

He finds 'efficient' ex-army men and offers them loads of money to do what they used to do, which was kill, harass and bully Iraqis and guard Mr Cheney's hamburgers as they are delivered by trucks to army bases.

For this he gets one thousand two hundred and sixty dollars an hour, waking and sleeping, seven days a week, all year round. Not from any available coffer of profits reaped by rape, pillage, ransom and looting as you might think, but from the US taxpayer.

For though his is a private army, the US government hires it, and pays big bucks for it.

Five hundred and ninety-three million dollars in 2006. Sixty-seven thousand eight hundred and eighty dollars every hour.

Big bucks it borrows from China and pays interest for.

61

Blackwater were in the headlines in 2007 when they opened fire at random 'without provocation' on a street corner in Baghdad and killed seventeen people 'including women and children' and wounded twenty-seven with machine guns and grenade launchers.

Nobody fired back, or fired first, and they were found to have acted culpably and were required to pay three thousand dollars each (on average) to the families they had bereaved.

On the five hundred and ninety-three million dollars a year they were getting they could afford this easily.

On one week's *interest* on this total they could pay the whole debt out.

Any privatisation is a licence to kill; discuss.

62

It is hard to see what good Blackwater is doing for the American people. The very memory of its name is an incitement to incendiary violence and suicide-bombing in Iraq, Iran and Pakistan and throughout the Arab world. It bespeaks with bloodstained eloquence American stupidity.

Yet the American government even under President Obama, though it's lately changed its name, a wise move, to 'Xe' (pronounce it if you can, I can't), has paid it until recently sixty-seven thousand eight hundred and eighty dollars *an hour* to continue its good work in Iraq.

63

It is not always as simple as this, of course.

There are as well part-privatisations, 'public-private part-nerships' (of which it has been wittily said, 'you socialise the losses and privatise the gains'), there are federal-state-and-private collusions in hospitals, football stadiums, harbour tunnels, Olympic Games and World Wars (in which Lockheed Air was paid lavish moneys to manufacture fighter planes by the Roosevelt government and was congratulated by the wily old cripple for its patriotic war profiteering, and IBM leased its punch-card system on a monthly basis to the Third Reich to facilitate the Holocaust).

And some of these collusions have merit. Some of them undoubtedly save lives, win wars and benefit mankind's future.

But there is one kind of privatisation that is corrupt at its heart and beyond contempt.

This is the privatisation of a government monopoly that *stays* a monopoly after it is sold.

64

It is the one that CEOs are most keen to get their hands on. An airport, an airline, a helicopter ambulance service, a century-old suburban railway service, a taxpayer-funded government bank or insurance company or housing-loan facility attracts them because of the lack of competition.

CEOs detest competition. Capitalism to them is not about competition, it's about the extermination of competition. They buy up, asset-strip and junk the competition. They crush with their might and their tactical mergers, Time-Life with Warner, Time Warner with Turner, Westinghouse with CBS, Seagram with Polygram, AOL with Time Warner Turner, Comcast with AT&T, General

Electric/NBC with Vivendi Universal, all the competition there is. They bring down prices till the small competitor goes broke, or sells out to them, and then put the prices up again. When he is gone they do what they like. That way they don't have to adhere to standards to do the right thing by the customers.

They set the standards now.

They want to erase all memory of previous standards.

They want to make *their* standards more 'efficient'.

They want to rewrite the book.

65

When Premier Greiner part-privatised the country trains of New South Wales he agreed with his new partners that the overnight sleeper services should be more 'efficient'.

There will be no more dining car, he decided, since this would cost three wages, no club car either, a further wage, and nevermore should the customer have the option to take his car on the train and drive it away on arrival at its tropical-coastal destination, a further wage.

Neither should there be any single sleeping compartments, since these multiplied the number of lavatories that had to be cleaned, and the quantity of onboard water required to flush them.

There would, however, be a new double-sleeper carriage with, aha, only one lavatory between four people.

A lavatory you had to enter by going out in the hall.

In my earlier book *First Abolish the Customer* I described the inconvenience of ten sleepless hours with whatever snoring and farting Scientologist you happened to be coupled with, and the repeated rigours of climbing down the ladder, dressing, going out in the hall, micturating, coming back, undressing, climbing the ladder, waking up your companion, arguing with him about the Book of Revelation and trying to sleep a few hours before you were woken at three a.m. and evicted onto a station where you waited forty minutes for a connecting bus to take you, at four a.m., to a beachside destination you used to, in pre-Greiner days, arrive at, having slept undisturbed all the way, at eight o'clock in the morning, rested and refreshed.

Worst were the eating arrangements, a queue for cardboard boxes in which warmed-over quiches, elderly chicken and superannuated pies were sold to you, and cans of half-strength beer lest you behave rowdily and cause the guards to throw you off the train at Taree.

Loudspeakers warned you not to drink to excess, or you would be 'put off at the next station', nor smoke in the toilets, for which you would be similarly punished.

You were (are) treated like potential criminals, not honoured guests; and this criminalisation, I suppose, is part and parcel of the 'efficiency' that comes with privatisation.

You can't afford to treat the customer well, you have to think of the bottom line. Sleep? Why does anybody need to sleep? In a *sleeping* compartment? Why?

The same logic would offer motel rooms without beds; if the customers agreed to stand up all night we could have more rooms, and more customers. More 'efficient' that way.

It's so efficient that the double sleepers are often empty, and the price of the journey has had to be doubled.

First abolish the customer, and keep on raising the bottom line.

You know it makes sense.

Economic fundamentalism declares it makes sense. And it is never wrong.

66

Who benefits from this? A few shareholders perhaps cheered by the bottom line.

Certainly not the CEO, whom a nation detests. Certainly not the miserable overworked railway guards-waiters-cooks-and-bedmakers, whom everybody snarls at. Certainly not the furtive smokers, put off in cold midnight at Coolongolook.

Does privatisation help or benefit society then?

No.

It doesn't, does it?

Why then do it?

Why then even contemplate it?

Why say over and over, 'There is no alternative'? TINA?

Who says that this is so?

THE RETURN OF SLAVERY

67

We have to contemplate the possibility that capitalism, or American capitalism at the very least, is a form of swindle; a con; a species of addictive drug sold by unscrupulous men to the unwary, the innocent, the ignorant and young.

Cigarettes, for instance, are sold to the young and they pay, on average, two hundred and fifty-six thousand dollars each for the forty-two years (my estimate) the poisonous habit takes to kill them, on average.

Unscrupulous men who themselves, as a rule, do not smoke, knowingly manufacture an addictive poison which fourteen-year-olds get hooked on, many of them girls who believe the poison will stop them from getting fat.

Which it does of course.

The excellent series *Mad Men* shows how early they knew their product was carcinogenic, and how diligently they connived, with bribed politicians and 'independent studies' and mendacious doctors, to conceal its toxicity, its danger to life, for its already-addicted customers.

They got Sir Laurence Olivier and Ronald Reagan and Kirk Douglas and Bing Crosby and Bob Hope and Fred Astaire and Lucille Ball and Lauren Bacall to advertise tobacco.

They claimed filters would reduce its 'harmful effects'.

They claimed their advertising campaigns (men on horseback, playboys on yachts or in speeding cars, cool young women in theatre foyers) were not aimed at children, just at people 'planning to change brands'.

About one hundred and sixty thousand Americans after 1955 died of lung cancer *every year*, and two hundred and forty thousand more from heart and liver and throat and other ailments brought on by two packs a day, including the Hollywood he-men Humphrey Bogart, John Wayne and Yul Brynner, or one thousand and ninety-five deaths a day for fifty years, a total of twenty million deaths by smoking, or three times the Holocaust, in America alone, and rather larger figures in the Third World.

When court cases were mounted to make W. D. & H. O. Wills pay for some of the deaths they had caused, executive after executive went into the dock and swore on oath, with hands raised, that they had 'never heard of any connection' between cigarette smoking and a range of illnesses.

I ask you to read that paragraph over again, and a few more times as well, and consider what it means.

68

It means, does it not, that the men of AIG who scarpered with their million-dollar payouts after wrecking the world, and the W. D. & H. O. Wills executives who peddled addictive poison to a hundred million teenage boys and girls and swore on oath that they weren't at the time aware that it was poisonous are not a few bad apples, or an exception to the rule, but what capitalism is all about.

Capitalism cheats and robs and kills and always has.

It has the ethic of the leopard and the jackal, the shark and the snake. It means us harm.

It robs our corpses and leaves us by the side of the road, our pockets ripped and emptied.

And Gordon Brown's plea for 'capitalism with a human face' is a Darwinian impossibility.

There never could, and never will be, such an evolutionary aberration.

For capitalism is about sacking people, and killing people, and hurting people, and tormenting people with the possibility of imminent poverty, and leaving them when the big bust comes to fend for themselves, and it isn't going to change.

69

A good example of this is James Hardie, the fibro company whose asbestos dust gave mesothelioma to at least five thousand Australians and whose lawyers strove for twenty years to stop them getting any money, any compensatory money at all, for their terrible suffering and early death. Four hundred and eighty-two of them died while the court case continued, including their feisty leader Bernie Banton, who in his last tortured, gasping week on earth got eight hundred thousand dollars for his trouble, though on the sixth-last day of his life the company tried to deny him all the money on the basis of a doctor's report made seven years before, and hidden.

70

Another is the famous case fought by Erin Brockovich in Hinkley, California, where six hundred and thirty-four people drank a good deal of the carcinogen Chromium 6 from a ground pool a mile wide and two miles long that the Pacific Gas and Electric Company's compressors had copiously polluted for a decade or so of cleaning the cooling towers with its toxicity. Three hundred and thirty-three million dollars, then a world-record settlement, was won by the litigants, many now deceased, though Erin and Ed Masry her ebullient employer (played in the film by Julia Roberts and Albert Finney) seized about half that sum for themselves in fees and expenses, and she's living well on the celebrity circuit now, compering television shows and giving speeches. Masry died four years ago, extremely rich.

Capitalism, even if defeated, offers side benefits to its

conquerors, who eventually, in this case anyway, join the system.

71

A similar mixture of toxic chemicals, deficient pipes, escaping water and workers ill-trained in emergency procedures or deficient in English killed sixteen thousand people in Bhopal, India, and injured five hundred and fifty thousand more, despite nine previous incidents affecting forty-seven other workers, one of them fatally, which the company ignored.

A vast gas cloud containing phosgene, hydrogen cyanide, carbon monoxide, hydrogen chloride, nitrous oxides, monomethyl amine and carbon dioxide caused coughing, vomiting, severe eye infections, a feeling of suffocation and a panic during which many people were trampled to death. Mass funerals followed, and mass cremations of bodies by the Narmada River. Two thousand dead bullocks and goats were buried. Leaves on trees went yellow and fell off. Three thousand pregnant women were affected, many miscarrying or having deformed infants.

The government of India took on the Union Carbide Corporation, an American firm, which offered three hundred and fifty million. Nonsense, said the government, we want three hundred and fifty *billion*.

Five years of bargaining followed and a settlement was reached of four hundred and seventy million, an average of, oh, three hundred and fifty dollars per victim, seven hundred and forty-five times *less* than what was asked for.

UCC's lawyers worked round the clock for five years to get the settlement sum down.

The CEO, Warren Anderson, who was initially arrested but was bailed and fled the country, earned just over eight hundred thousand dollars in the year of the disaster, and gave none of it back.

72

Capitalism kills people and isn't very interested in paying for its crimes. It prefers to get away with them, and retain on staff 'administrators' whose principal purpose is to hose down embittered complainants and cover up crimes against humanity.

73

Such men did their work well when the Beaconsfield mine in Northern Tasmania caved in, killing Larry Knight and imprisoning, famously, in a small dark space Todd Russell and Brant Webb for fourteen days while the world watched, absorbed by their good cheer, foul jokes and defecatory inconveniences.

Though responsible for the cave-in and for Larry's death – miners' warnings of the mine props' instability and previous tremors had not convinced them to make costly repairs – they responded to the disaster by forcibly

retrenching, after union negotiations, eleven mine workers and no executives.

What an above-ground executive does in a gold mine is
hard to imagine.

The men dig out the gold, at the risk of their lives.

What does the executive do?

Count it, probably.

Say no to an extra tea break.

No wonder he's worth two hundred and fourteen thousand dollars a year.

What a hard job that is.

74

Is capitalism a freedom-friendly system? In Guatemala,
El Salvador, Chile, Iran and South Korea it seems not.
There were coups in these democratic countries that
installed right-wing dictators and a Shah in the 1950s,
'60s and '70s, all backed by the US State Department, the
US Marines, the CIA or United Fruit, newspapers closed
down, dissidents tortured and the wages of the average
worker reduced to a few dollars a day, sometimes two,
sometimes ten.

In capitalism's pet country Israel, which does have a
free press and violently contradictory editorials, several
Arab parties are banned from seeking parliamentary election and opposition figures killed in their beds, mosques
or city streets and their widows' houses bulldozed.

In capitalist Russia journalists and broadcasters are assassinated, rival politicians gaoled or, in Mikhail Gorbachev's case, banned from being interviewed on broadcast television, elections are rigged and the rules they are run by lately changed so one man, Putin, currently fifty-six, can rule in perpetuity.

75

There are, however, considerable freedoms in Britain, Ireland, France, Germany, Austria and Spain but these are scarcely capitalist states. They are to varying extents all 'mixed economies' or 'social democracies' (more correctly called 'the social market') and all regulated by the stern rules of the European Union, a giant supranational conspiracy of subsidised need and shared wealth.

76

Is 'extreme neo-liberalism' then (I quote Australian Prime Minister Kevin Rudd) encouraging of democratic freedoms?

No. It is more like Italian fascism, whose direct philosophical descendant, according to the eminent philosopher John Ralston Saul in his book *Voltaire's Bastards*, is Corporatism.

It's the system George W. Bush believed in, and so did his grandfather Prescott Bush, who made a lot of money out of German armaments factories and helped fund the promising politician Adolf Hitler's rise to power.

How then are 'freedom' and 'capitalism' said in the same breath?

It probably goes back to the Boston Tea Party, when certain freedom-loving tea planters, resentful of tariffs, filled up Boston Harbor with barrels of tea.

'Freedom from onerous tax' got mixed up that night with freedom in general and the Americans have got the two things mixed up ever since.

The freedom they fought for – and won – included the freedom to own slaves (which their foes the British were planning to abolish) and thus led Abraham Lincoln, eighty years on, to say that freedom must not go so far as to include the freedom to oppress.

For then it is freedom only for some, and not others.

77

International corporate capitalism is 'the freedom to oppress'; discuss.

When it's unregulated, it is.

Was Abraham Lincoln a free-market capitalist or a social democrat?

A social democrat, I'd say.

He didn't believe in slaves.

All the signatories of the Declaration of Independence owned slaves, but he didn't. And he didn't believe in owning slaves.

78

This leads us to the difficult, absorbing, upsetting question: *What, then, does economic fundamentalism have to do with democracy? Is there any connection between these two concepts? Any connection at all?*

Hardly any, it would currently seem.

Economic fundamentalist theoreticians oppose the existence of unions, and want them out of the workplace, and preferably off the earth. They resent the existence of governments, and any rule they exert over the global workings of their international, predatory enterprises. They hate paying a penny in compensation to people their work conditions bereave or kill. They fight like beavers to restrict and reduce the rights and rewards of people they suddenly sack. They like to deal with governments in countries where factory workers get, as they used to in Guatemala, twenty-four cents a day.

They yearn for workers' conditions that are pretty much like slavery, and prefer to set up shop in countries where this is more likely.

79

Slavery wasn't all bad.

A slave had a roof, and a wife, and home-cooked meals and children, though these children might be sold off to another owner at fourteen.

He could sing and play the banjo with his fellow

slaves and secretly practise by midnight his voodoo religion while praying and singing in Christian congregations, restricted by colour, in wooden churches in the daytime.

His wife could form bonds with those white children she raised as their 'mammy' and the various white men who raped her and made her pregnant, and sent off, like Jefferson, her mulatto children into lifelong unreturning exile far from his sight.

His own sons. Think of that.

Potential geniuses. Just like that.

Slavery was the usual practice in most systems throughout history, including Judea's brief rule of Jerusalem's environs in the tenth BCE, and Athens' Golden Age.

In America it's a time that is looked back on with fondness, as its two most attended movies *Gone with the Wind* and *The Birth of a Nation* show, and the flying still, even now, of the Confederate flag over many Southern porches. And the American mindset that for three hundred years kept slaves, and whipped and raped them, castrated them if they were impertinent, cut off a hand now and then, was alive and well in international corporate America, seeking child slaves and factory slaves and peasant farmers on slave wages in other lands.

The average wage United Fruit paid Central American workers in the fifties was twenty-four cents a day. The average wage a United Fruit executive gave himself, though he picked no fruit nor canned it, nor carried it to market, was, probably, five hundred thousand dollars a year, or thirteen hundred and sixty-nine dollars a day. United Fruit itself made five hundred million dollars a year in the early 1950s, which is six and a half billion dollars in our money now, and its annual net earnings were greater then than the GDP of any of the Central American countries in which it grew its bananas.

80

Slavery is in the genes of capitalism, you might say.

Much corporate wealth in America was built on it (as Michael Moore unwelcomely pointed out in *Bowling for Columbine*) and its use overseas of compliant, perspiring wage slaves – in the opium fields of Afghanistan, the sugar-cane plantations of Haiti – was infamous, reviled and constant in the latter half of the twentieth century.

In the 1990s, however, and the early twenty-first century, came a new kind of slavery.

81

Bank clerks, in their millions, were replaced by ATMs, devices in shopping malls and pubs and city centres that dispensed money. These wondrous, inexpensive robots worked round the clock, received no wages, no pension benefits nor holiday pay.

At midnight or noon they were equally deferential

(often showing a nice smiling young woman on the screen) and, along with telephone and internet banking, have been responsible for the loss of forty thousand jobs in Australia alone.

With the money saved from having to pay fewer people and the money made from ATM charges, the bank CEO was able to invest in subprime mortgages, hedge funds, mineral exploration and the air fares of bank officers (those who still had jobs) to rove the earth looking for profit-making businesses to buy up cheap in impoverished countries, or government monopolies in their own.

Because the robot-slave cost very little to maintain – it required only two men with a truckload of money to occasionally replenish it and an accountant at head office to add up what, in fees, it had lately earned – it allowed the CEO to pay himself, well, thirty-three million a year (or sixty-two dollars seventy-nine cents a minute, awake or asleep) in the case of Macquarie Bank in 2007, and 13.9 million a year in the case of the head of AIG, twenty-six dollars forty-five cents a minute, day and night, including weekends.

Like the Virginia tobacco planter of 1830 or the white Kenyan tea planter of 1910, the bank CEO does well out of underpaid labour.

The antebellum Southern slave made, in modern terms, food and rent thrown in, thirteen dollars a day, the tea-picking coolie of the British Empire in the early twentieth century, fifteen dollars a day.

The ATM costs rather more than that, forty dollars a day for servicing and maintenance. But it does the work of (roughly) seven slaves, which would, if you had a mind to adding these things up, bring its comparable cost down to six dollars a day.

Which is cheaper than slavery.

And probably more efficient.

82

The use of mechanised robot-assistants on cotton farms, auto assembly lines, clothing factories, open-cut coal mines and newspaper printing works meant CEOs could sack scores of millions of humans from jobs which they and their forebears had done for centuries.

The chattering girls at the telephone exchange like the one recreated in *Changeling* vanished. Likewise the grim-faced women from the railway cafes, replaced by Coke machines. Half the men and women who sold train tickets went with them, and all the teenage bus and tram conductors, their work done by machines that gulp and cough up bits of irradiated plastic, machines that cost the profit-hungry corporation two percent, maybe, of what the humans they usurped once earned for similar menial work, to pay their way through college.

83

This process which we might call the Return of Slavery has not only enriched the CEOs beyond the dreams of Croesus, it has also scared the bejesus out of the workers, now competing with slaves on two fronts, mechanical at home and human overseas, into accepting lower and lower wages.

In the Bush years the minimum wage for a time was five dollars fifteen cents an hour in jobs that many people worked at only twelve or fourteen hours a week and the phrase 'working poverty' entered the language.

A more frank, more honest combination of words is 'situational slavery'.

84

For though the worker (a single black mother, say, with a child and a job as a cloakroom attendant from seven p.m. to eleven p.m. three nights a week) can theoretically quit and move on – and seek work, say, as an opera star on forty times her present wage at the Met – in real life she is terrified out of her mind, like an assistant kitchenmaid at Tara, under the cool green gaze of her mistress Scarlett O'Hara.

Slavery as we see it now, 'situational slavery', is absence of real choice in how we spend our lives and feed our children.

And more and more humans, menaced by the

remorseless advance of robots into jobs they used to do, live lives of less and less choice and more and more desperation, as the CEOs remove them at a moment's notice, and send them on their way with pittances, or fight court cases to deny them every dollar owed to them by 'natural justice' and thus gratify the Superpersons whose share values creep up with every sacking.

They apply for other work, do a hundred and four interviews and get nowhere.

Eventually they accept work cleaning toilets or hoovering offices from midnight to dawn, and another similar job elsewhere from eight till five.

They are too tired to enjoy their children, and snap at their wife when she rejects a drunken caress, between shifts, at seven a.m. She has a job herself cleaning hotel rooms, and she needs her sleep.

And the mortgage repayment rates go up by fifty dollars a week in a month, and they have to assess what food they eat.

If this isn't slavery, or situational slavery, I'm keen to know what you would call it.

85

It is worth asking at this point whether slavery, or situational slavery (SS), is good for the economy.

Or as good for the economy as it was in the days of Simon Legree.

A human being in a state of 'working poverty' doesn't consume much.

Little of the income of, say, a twenty-nine-year-old black single mother in Cleveland with two kids and a jobless visiting abusive lover goes on luxury goods.

She spends little on perfume, haircuts, designer jeans, leg-waxes or shoes. She eats out barely ever. Any spare money she has her lover spends on drink and cigarettes.

She contributes to no health fund, no opera season, no ride at Coney Island, no package tour to Florida and Disney World with her children.

Any help she is to the economy is marginal, and if she uses food stamps, or spends time in gaol, she is a drain on the public purse.

If her twelve-year-old son starts pushing drugs, moreover, the cost to the public purse of her 'situational slavery' increases.

And we might begin to wonder if slavery is worth the money we spend on it.

86

This is not just a joke line but a way of looking at the cost of 'working poverty' to a society.

And the cost of 'economic rationalism', or economic fundamentalism, to the way money trickles down in that society.

A man loses his job collecting money on a bridge when

a computer system of held-up cards and flashing lights replaces him.

He goes on a bender and on the fourth night crashes his car and writes it off.

Slightly injured, he spends two days in hospital.

He has already cost his insurers four thousand two hundred dollars.

He goes on unemployment relief drawing, say, two hundred and thirty dollars a week from the public purse.

He continues to drink and one night in an argument knocks his wife out and breaks the cheekbone of his daughter who intervenes.

The police are called and he and his wife are made to undergo compulsory counselling, costing the public services, probably, eight hundred dollars more.

This fails to help. He beats her again, and she flees with her six-year-old son and ten-year-old daughter to a women's refuge, costing the state more money, two hundred dollars perhaps, for her temporary accommodation.

A divorce ensues, the subprime-mortgaged house is sold at a loss, which costs the bank sixty thousand dollars, and soon in alcoholic despair our man, call him Joe, acquires a gun and holds up a petrol station, is arrested and sentenced to four years.

It costs the state eighty-two dollars a day for the two and a half years he serves to accommodate and feed him in gaol.

The cost of that one sacking is now six hundred and twenty thousand dollars. This is more than he would have earned, from the job he no longer has, in thirteen years.

87

It may be argued that this is a rare and particular case, that it doesn't happen to many people who are sacked and shamed and impoverished, their self-concept wounded, their hopes blighted.

But every one of them is traumatised, and so are their families, and few respond to trauma very well.

In America thirty thousand deaths by gunfire occur every year, that is, more than three per hour. And seventeen thousand of these are suicides. Very few of them were gainfully employed.

So it could be argued that sacking is the triggering mechanism in many early American deaths, and 'situational suicides', perhaps no more than ten thousand a year.

But the 13.5 billion dollars these ten thousand dead people might have earned, and contributed to the economy in the following thirty years, if they had *not* been sacked, is a sizeable figure.

So how can it be said, at this point, that economic fundamentalism, whose principal tool is the sacking of humans and their replacement by machines or overseas slave labour, adds up when the true cost is computed, the cost to the nation, the society, and the sum of human happiness, out of which an economy grows?

How can you say that?

88

It's even less likely you can say it when you look at the figures attendant on a single sacking, what John Maynard Keynes called 'the multiplier effect'.

As I argued in my 1998 book *First Abolish the Customer*, when you sack one person, you lose four customers, four customers at least, who can no longer afford to buy the goods you sell.

And the man, his wife and two children will no longer like your brand name and will not buy your product.

Nor will his mother, father and mother-in-law.

Nor will *they* buy much else but mincemeat and spaghetti in the average week as they pitch in to help the sacked man's family.

Products like new designer shoes, hundred-dollar jeans or first-hand Chrysler cars will be out of the reach for the first time of these helpful people, since the sacking has cost them each in turn so much.

If a thousand workers in the one town are sacked from the same factory this means four, six, seven thousand blood relatives are, by this 'multiplier effect', likewise diminished in their power to buy things. Economically disabled. Financially hobbled.

And the sackings begin to spread – like swine flu – through the economy.

Eighty houses go on sale in the one town, after the sackings, at the one time.

And the house prices plummet, and some houses are abandoned, and become derelict, and six hundred, perhaps, of the children of the sacked resentful workers drift towards criminality.

And the infection spreads.

Like swine flu. Like SARS. Like the Black Plague.

89

This is how, we are told, the system 'works', employers taking 'rational' decisions to 'downsize' (where once they expanded) their companies, and retrenched, impoverished workers taking 'rational decisions' to seek work 'in another sector of the economy'.

But it *costs* the economy dearly, in goods not bought, in money not earned and spent by the thirteen retrenched workers in a thousand who suicide, by the early cancer deaths of those teenage girls who, stressed, grow fat from comfort-eating and take up smoking at fifteen to bring down their weight and get hooked.

A sacking in a one-factory town is a terrible thing; discuss.

A sacking in a one-factory town is a terrorist act; discuss.

An act of economic terrorism.

90

It abolishes the customer.

And it sometimes sends him crazy.

91

Many, many shopping-mall massacres, or schoolhouse massacres, or church-congregation massacres, are carried out by young men who have lately been 'let go' or 'laid off' or are ending their school or college years and see ahead of them no chance of worthwhile future employment.

Their pride has been smashed, and they end, like suicide bombers, by attacking and killing their neighbours, a small and frantic and pitiful equivalent of blowing up the world.

92

Only connect, as E. M. Forster once said.

Only connect.

93

In Sweden, whose sacked workers are treated mercifully, and do not have to sell their dwelling, interrupt their children's lives, or move in with their mother-in-law and drown their sorrows in cheap drink, the number of deaths by gunfire is about two hundred and twenty per year.

In America in 2006, *before* the crash, it was thirty thousand per year.

Adjusted to population that is 2.27 deaths per hundred thousand people by gunfire each year in Sweden, versus 9.86 per hundred thousand in the USA.

Economic fundamentalism, as I have said before, kills people and social democracy saves, or tends to save, lives.

94

Economic fundamentalism adds up only if you do not count the dead. Discuss.

Or, to paraphrase Bob Dylan, 'You don't count the dead when money's on your side.'

Discuss.

95

The thirty thousand killed by gunfire every year in the USA, and the two hundred thousand relatives and friends thus traumatised and in need of 'counselling' means a lot more money is not spent on shoes and designer jeans and champagne by the families required to pay for the funerals and the psychiatric hospitalisation.

Had there been no culture of sacking, nicknamed 'economic rationalism', and no glamorous fashion of paying CEOs, day and night, thirty dollars a minute, there would have been more money in the capitalist system, prospering more people who would buy, as customers, more goods.

But 'economic rationalism' knew better. It sacked three

thousand people in the one town, and set the swine flu going.

And the bullets flying.

And the scared, scarred people leaving town and seeking more slave-work in other towns, other counties, other states.

Prepared to do the same work for less money.

And live on mince and packet spaghetti.

Till a machine replaces them too.

It's called the Return of Slavery; discuss.

96

And in order to compete with slavery, we have to become slaves ourselves; discuss.

97

There is on top of this, I should probably add, what I call SCS, or Self-Chosen Slavery.

The volunteer football coach, the woman who decides to stay home to look after her Down Syndrome baby, the volunteer fire-fighter, lifesaver, bandmaster, the amateur theatre director, the church choirmaster, the unpaid reader of books to the blind, the eight-year-old helping out in the shop, disrupt with their self-chosen slavery (all right, all right, call it *goodness*) the economy as surely as far-off Taiwanese clothing workers on a dollar an hour.

They distort our view of things, and make it easier for

governments not to pay parents a weekly wage for child-rearing, or give them four hundred and eighty days off (as Sweden does) to get through breast-feeding, potty-training and the first marvellous months of language-learning on full pay.

Slavery is particularly ingrained in large families who run shops or farms, and gives an economic advantage to Muslims and Catholics with big, cooperative, conspiratorial extended families.

Volunteerism of this and other sorts (volunteers, for instance, were much of the goodwill factor as guides in the Sydney Olympics) is a constant ingredient of all cultures, all societies, all religions, all political systems.

How then can we have a level playing field now, or ever? We can't.

It's a flat-earth theory; another flat-earth theory, like many before it.

Discuss.

THE TRUE CURRENCY
OF THE WORLD

98

It has been said that God, who has thus far killed since Cro-Magnon times eight billion of us, loves us very much.

So much so that he ordered the torture and murder of his own son, in order that these eight billion souls, already dead, would not *necessarily* also fry in hell.

If we agreed that his lunacy was a good idea, and if we 'submitted to his will', we would come *back* from the dead and bow down at his feet and sing hymns in his praise and gambol by glassy streams, and fondle sleepy lions and eat vegetarian food for all eternity.

This crazed sales pitch has won over a lot of people in the past nineteen hundred years of disembowelled, unrepentant Jews and Protestant and Catholic zealots burnt at the stake for minor disagreements over doctrine (whether Mary died a virgin and ascended directly into heaven without any intervening days in Purgatory, whether angels had sexual organs, how many angels could dance on the head of a pin, and so on), people who called themselves True Believers, members of the One True Faith, the Communion of Saints, the one-hundred-and-forty-four-thousand, the Chosen Elect.

Over two billion people, dead and living, have bought holus-bolus some variant of this doctrine of Redemption, based on the sacrificial torture and slaughter of a Son of God, who *pays out* our debt to the deity by suffering in our stead.

Margaret Atwood in her recent book *Payback: Debt and the Shadow Side of Wealth* points out that this instinctual, reflexive belief in debt repayment runs deep in the tribes of the west who all sacrificed bullocks, virgins, doves and captured foes to soothe the tempers of their various jealous gods and thus ensured good crops, an absence of storms, infections, plagues, and so on, in millenniums past.

In the Bible, Abraham proposes to sacrifice Isaac, his only legitimate son, born to a wife already a hundred years old and destined to father the Jewish and Arab peoples, including Woody Allen and me, because God in a dream told him to, and is just about to do it when God changes his mind.

Whew.

His cousin Lot offers his virgin daughters to a roaring mob of Sodomites who are keen to have sex with two visiting angels, a sacrifice to his notion of worshipful hospitality. 'Take my daughters instead,' he bargains with these bad men.

Jephthah cuts the throat of his daughter because he promised God if he won a particular big battle he would sacrifice the first creature that greeted him when he came home.

He regretfully tells his daughter what he has to do, and she *agrees to this*, submits to his need to keep his sacred vow, asking only that she be allowed a fortnight to go to the hills and 'bewail her virginity' before she comes back and submits to God's will, and her father's knife, according to his bargain with the deity.

Agamemnon in *The Iliad* sacrifices his daughter Iphigenia in order to ensure fair winds and good sailing of his triremes to Troy.

In Shakespeare's *Measure for Measure*, Isabella is asked to sacrifice her virginity to save her brother from being hanged (and, controversially, refuses to).

In Dickens's *A Tale of Two Cities*, Sydney Carton goes to the guillotine in the stead of his lookalike rival Charles Darnay to expiate the sins of his own louche, drunken life and win back the love of his adored, lost Lucie Manette posthumously.

In Hemingway's *For Whom the Bell Tolls*, Robert Jordan, well aware the battle is lost, nonetheless stays behind to fight it, knowing that by his sacrifice his beloved Maria will be able to escape.

These stories of bargains struck and traded lives populate our literature, and our national myths as well.

The eight thousand one hundred and fifty-nine Australians sacrificed at Gallipoli in a battle lost in the first day and protracted for eight months were said to have been worth it for they showed Australia had 'come of age'.

The six thousand eight hundred Americans dead on Iwo Jima in a four-week battle, which proved to be needless five months later when Hiroshima and Nagasaki were bombed and an unconditional surrender signed, were immortalised as heroes by a photo of a flag being raised, whose sacrifice showed America would 'pay any price, bear any burden', to save the world from fascist colonisation.

It was likewise thought that John McCain who was hung up by his broken shoulders and 'kicked in the nuts' and otherwise tortured for five and a half years in Vietnam, and refused to go home when his captors offered him the chance to do so because 'it wasn't my turn', had earned the Presidency by his suffering in a war that was lost, and pointless, and wasted 4.5 million lives.

His brave sacrifice was a fair deposit on the White House, it was reasoned, though he had shown himself to be incompetent in battle, and also in captivity when he finally and fraudulently confessed he was indeed a war criminal, and was allowed to go home.

99

Sacrifice, redemption, guilt and payback seem to be written into our genes. We 'make sacrifices' for our children. We die for our country. We take on lifelong mortgages. We pay as we go. We do not pass on our debts to our children. We die possessed of the house they grew up in.

In the various myths attendant on the Mafia, in Hollywood films and paperback novels, the owed favour is the true currency of the world. You hand over the man we want, we'll hand over the man you want.

Barack Obama's African grandfather paid fifteen cows for his young virgin bride, and when she found him unpleasant to be with, and ran away and returned to her family, he demanded, and got, the fifteen cows back and kept the baby she had borne him, Barack Obama Senior.

By this savage barter we acquired the present leader of the world.

100

Somewhere along the way these trading arrangements, these assessed values of a bride's maidenhead, a god's forgiveness, a saint's intercession, a kidnapped monarch's life expressed in square miles of a kingdom yielded up as ransom to his conqueror, came to be expressed in money.

Money, as in St Paul's great sentence about faith, is the substance of things hoped for, the evidence of things not seen.

It was a portable means of exchange for a man who could not, say, bring all his elephants conveniently to market but could bring half the *price* of them in a bag, in assurance of their eventual delivery.

Money became the way things happened.

An attractive metal, gold, came to express its value.

(Or, in the Andes, an attractive tasty confectionery, chocolate.)

And at some point it was discovered that money could be considered to have value *in itself*, and it could be lent out at interest.

Jesus overturned the tables of the 'money-changers' (that is, the currency traders) in the Temple, and caused such annoyance to the priests and capitalists that he was crucified eight days later for it.

It is not known what angrily disputed rate of exchange or interest he died for, a mighty sacrifice indeed.

Julius Caesar funded his political career, the payment of street gangs, and chefs for public banquets, and so on, with more and more loans that paid back former loans at higher and higher rates of interest.

The noble Brutus lent money to the Salaminians at forty-eight percent.

This idea, that a means of exchange can have value *in itself*, concentrated wonderfully the minds of the greedy, as it does in this century too.

101

A means of exchange, the credit card, attracts near-Brutus levels of additional earnings, eighteen percent on the money owed, plus *two dollars* seized by the ATM on each transaction (that is, about two hundred and sixty dollars per customer per annum) if it is not your bank but another.

Insurance premiums, moreover, of perhaps five hundred dollars a year are paid against burglary, fire and car accident, things that if they occasionally happen rarely cost the customer that much. The car insurance is particularly wicked since you pay the *first five hundred's worth* of the damages yourself.

Since the damage often doesn't exceed five hundred (a smashed rear windscreen, a broken headlight), you pay for the accident twice.

All this, of course, is the only way to run a society.

There is no alternative; discuss.

102

It was long known that land is money, of course, that you could rent it out to another and still own it, and raise the rent, remorselessly, from time to time and the share-farmer thus pauperised would have no option but to pay you more.

But it came to be known some time in the early twentieth century that time is money too.

The government-run telephone services found they could charge a shilling for a three-minute long-distant call on a public phone, and more if the time was extended.

This price inflated over a century to twenty-five cents a local call *despite the sacking of all the telephone girls and their replacement by machines,* or forty-seven cents a minute if you wanted to ring London, *though the robots who put you through worked no harder, nor cost no less if you never called at all.*

Then came privatisation, and the telcos discovered a new trick.

This was to charge you for time you hadn't asked for.

This new swindle occurs when you get through to a number that isn't answering, and a female voice then says, 'The person you have called is not available. At the tone, record your message. To end, simply hang up, or wait for further options.'

This takes ten seconds and costs most mobile owners twenty-two cents more than they would otherwise have paid. This adds up, over a year, to two hundred and nineteen million dollars (at a fair guess) filched from Australia's economy or three billion five hundred and four million from America's economy.

This money could have been better spent – on, say, piping Niugini's Fly River into the Darling and saving Australia's orchard and farm industries.

Or sustaining seventy small theatre companies for a thousand years on the interest alone.

One mustn't get too angry or contemptuous over small matters, but it's been common knowledge for over a century that one may terminate a phone call by 'simply hanging up'.

And you don't need to be told this.

A one-second bell-sound and a voice saying 'send message now' would have sufficed.

And saved Australia a hundred and fifty million dollars a year.

103

The length of that message helped pay Sol Trujillo the thirty-one million dollars plus the Telstra shares he walked away with.

It is the contention of this book that this money could have been better spent.

On keeping in work for, say, five years, twelve hundred of the telephone linesmen and telephone repairmen he sacked, for instance, and saving their families from the trauma and disruption of leaving their country towns.

104

Even greater, though, in these chronicles of lost time, and the money we pay for it, are the charges made for six hours in a Sydney parking station.

A grimy patch of concrete, five feet wide and twelve feet long, no bigger than a cell in Guantanamo, accrues for a five-hour stay in some Sydney buildings, and you have to be out by nine p.m., sixty-eight dollars.

This is the price of a ticket to *Guys and Dolls* and offers a good deal less enjoyment.

In a day the one parking station – call it, for argument's sake, the one in Macquarie Towers – earns, when three-quarters full, eight thousand seven hundred and forty-eight dollars, and in a five-day week, forty-three thousand seven hundred and forty dollars, and, in a year, two million two hundred and seventy-four thousand four hundred dollars or thereabouts. (This is my estimate and may vary from the actual figure by ten or twenty thousand dollars.)

Its upkeep is minimal. A security guard and a single man are there on standby, each costing, perhaps, thirty-five thousand a year, in case the automatic boom ceases to work, and cleaners costing half that come in once a month to hose it down.

And the carpark earns in a year three million dollars more than Van Gogh did in a lifetime out of painting (figures adjusted for inflation), and this is thought to be a fair and reasonable variety of capitalist enterprise.

The CEO of Wilson Parking, which owns forty-six Sydney parking stations, pays himself (probably) 2.5 million a year, that is, two hundred and eighty-five dollars an hour, round the clock, including Sundays and holidays . . . To do what?

What does he do to fill in his time?

Contemplate on his yacht, drinking Moët I suppose, his well-deserved, ongoing and pleasurable equivalent of the Divine Right of Kings.

105

There are further examples of these unearned greedy profits throughout most modern, western societies. A charge by Australian Customs of thirty-five dollars to enter the country. A charge of six dollars an hour to park in a beachside reserve. A charge, by the minute, of a lawyer for taking your call.

A charge of thirty thousand dollars a year for three years for a university degree for someone whose parents, in a time of Australian social democracy, got one for no down payment and a good deal of subsidised hard study, and paid the nation back in taxes.

106

The author once co-owned with his wife a small theatre, seating capacity a hundred and twenty-five, and charged four hundred dollars a week for the rent of it, an equivalent in today's terms of maybe fourteen hundred dollars a week.

It now costs one thousand dollars a night.

A rival theatre a mile away costs eight thousand dollars a night.

This makes it very hard to put on plays, and for the forty good actors who graduate each year from Sydney's drama courses to earn a living.

They go into bar-tending and hotel management and taxi-driving.

Young people as gifted as Russell Crowe, Cate Blanchett, Mel Gibson or Nicole Kidman are not, as they should be, winning Oscars but, in Dustin Hoffman's famous Oscar-accepting words, 'practising accents while driving a taxi'.

Is wasting great actors good for the economy?

Who then is it good for? A few theatre landlords? Is that all?

A few theatre landlords? Really? No-one else?

Can it be stopped?

107

Quite easily actually.

But we probably shouldn't discuss that yet.

Lest we be thought over-radical in what we believe; or what we grimly, ferociously, logically advocate.

108

What is clear, though, is not just that Dick Fuld, the CEO of Lehman Brothers, was paid too much, an average of thirty-three million dollars a year, for wrecking the world economy – since it was his company that was the critical ingredient in the economic carnage (of which, as Gordon Brown says, 'four hundred thousand more children will die') – but that he was pretty mad to *want* so much.

What can you do with the total he racked up, five hundred million dollars? Apart from banking it, and getting as *interest* on it, day and night, two thousand eight hundred and fifty-three thousand dollars an hour? From the interest alone?

You can only eat three meals a day, sleep in one bed, steer one yacht, fly one private jet at a time.

What do you do with the five hundred million dollars, or the five hundred million one thousand since you started reading this chapter?

What crazed impulse makes you want money like that? What crazed impulse makes your shareholders want to give it to you?

109

My wife informs me it is to do with male pride.

If a man's rival gets twenty million a year, he wants twenty-two million a year. It's a measure of his status, and it makes him feel better.

Even if it results in the destruction, or contributes to the destruction, of Lehman's and the world economy.

And the death of four hundred thousand children, two hundred thousand of them from Africa.

Potential Barack Obamas, some of them, sacrificed in infancy to one man's greed.

Or four hundred men's greed.

110

Should this tedious arithmetic of infant death and corporate avarice matter? This dreary computation of blood and gold?

Or is it not worth saying, is it somehow impertinent to bring up, the moral cost and the practical cost of neo-liberal capitalism in the post-Reagan–Thatcher years?

Should we just stay calm, be quiet and not raise the inequity of things?

Should we teach ourselves, as T. S. Eliot advises, to keep still, and let the Superpersons creep away with the swag? With the earnings, over a lifetime, of more ordinary, more responsible, more decent human beings?

Is it time we simply just surrendered, and called out in chorus:

'There is no alternative!'

THIS GUY IS A LOSER

111

We have seen how social-democrat societies and some communist societies kill fewer infants, nourish more children, educate more adolescents, provide more doctors and give better health care and old-age care to adults and sick people and people in twilight homes than economic fundamentalist societies, and how the economic fundamentalist societies over-reward – by scores of millions a year sometimes – the unrepentant killers of the newborn, hungry and poor when a fraction of the current wages of western CEOs would cleanse the water and reduce the smoking habits and the chronic drunkenness of millions of the starving and unmedicated in Africa and the Subcontinent.

It is appropriate we should ask at this point not why the economic fundamentalists do it (they are mostly male, proud and crazy) but why so many western societies – the United States in particular – have accepted without caveat this greedy, punishing ethic, the code of the roving hyena, they live by.

It is to do, I think, with the skill of their propaganda.

112

In their many media and advertising campaigns they say it is the *politicians* who are the greedy ones, not they.

These politicians are only in it for the money.

On a mind-boggling one hundred and seventeen thousand dollars a year plus some free travel these unprincipled swine work sixteen, eighteen hours a day absorbing the woes of crazed constituents and enduring long nights of ethnic dancing because they *love the money they get for it*, and for no other reason, the bastards, while the selfless CEO *on thirty times that amount* wants only to serve the needs of his much more deserving shareholders.

They have embedded this nasty idea in the public mind with great persuasive skill through countless newspaper stories and bellicose fulminations by radio and cable-TV commentators.

And they have gone after the union movement in the same way. The union 'bosses' are 'rorting the system', they say, bleeding their fuddled membership of enormous unearned salaries for themselves and 'kickbacks' for their 'cronies', all of whom 'care little' for the needs of 'ordinary working people', and earn as much as *two hundred thousand dollars a year*, the unprincipled greedy swine. They have 'their noses forever in the trough'.

In an act of propaganda brilliance, they have lately made sure that the word 'boss' applies only to union leaders, not the captains of industry or those in charge of gigantic money-trading corporations, who bear the much softer-sounding title CEO.

Back when *they* were called bosses (and were shown in cartoons as big-bellied moustachioed cigar-smoking top-hatted buffoons holding tiny shrivelled workers in their tightening grasp) they were much more *visibly* evil and the term CEO, Chief Executive Officer, which suggests a quietly-spoken mild-mannered servant-of-the-public-good who never sacks anybody, was crafted as a substitute.

The masters of propaganda never target *him* – we have to pay him that much, they say, or we'd lose him to a better offer overseas. But they do go after small-time crooks whom they stalk and harass on their current affairs programmes, people who sometimes swindle widows of forty or fifty thousand dollars.

Never the twenty-one thousand nine hundred and seven dollars a CEO makes in a day and whether he deserves this, and what he gets it for.

And they've come up with a very useful concept.

A Big Lie, some might call it.

This is the concept of the 'loser'.

113

Most Americans have come to believe, in part because of the films and the television series they watch, that some people are 'winners' and some people are 'losers'.

A loser is going to lose whatever the social conditions

he grows up in. In *Seinfeld* he is George Costanza, forever testing his employers with his impertinence and losing his job, forever saying the wrong thing to the parents of his girlfriends.

In *The Simpsons* he is Barney, the shouting, tottering drunk. In *South Park* he is Kenny, who through eerie misfortune gets killed in every episode.

A loser is not always a bad person, but he is cursed by fate. The trailer-trash family of Maggie Fitzgerald the heroine of *Million Dollar Baby* are examples of this. They cannot even steal money from their paralysed daughter (who has millions) with any efficiency.

What is to be done with losers? Well, there are ways to help them out, to turn them, with difficulty, into winners.

This often involves physical torture, which is no less than they deserve.

Rocky is put through rigorous training, including punching sides of meat, in order that he has a chance of beating Apollo Creed, the world heavyweight champion, or coming close to beating him, in an exhibition match in 1976, America's bicentennial year. He does well, and is redeemed.

Fast Eddie Felson, a skilful pool player brought low by drink, overweening pride and sex before marriage (and some low-down hoons who break his thumbs) in *The Hustler* is redeemed by the girl's suicide, 'gets character' he calls it, and finally, in a thirty-hour game, beats Minnesota Fats and is banned from playing high-class pool forever. Once a loser, always a loser, it seems, in his case.

The definition of loser, unfortunately, has widened since the 1970s, when it first took hold, to include most of American society.

A loser is now that man or woman who is not yet taking home a million a year, is not CEO of Time Warner or General Motors or the star, on twenty million dollars a film, of the *Lethal Weapon* or *Die Hard* franchise and is not, like Donald Trump, making squillions and saying 'You're fired' to this week's apprentice, a talented loser who like Fast Eddie Felson lacks the last few inches of the Right Stuff, of Character, and thus, found wanting, must go back to the provinces and redeem himself, if he can, in the eyes of his greedy wife and mortified old father.

By this rigorous measurement, it seems, ninety-eight percent of Americans are losers, and they take it badly when this is indicated to them, when they are fired or fail to gain entrance to a university or a Broadway chorus line.

They buy a gun from a gun shop and shoot many of their neighbours or fellow students crying 'Call me a loser will you, motherfucker? You're the one who's losing!'

Then turn the gun on themselves.

114

The appellation works well for capitalism because it absolves the system from the need to help people out. These people are 'unredeemable' and those who do not succumb to drug overdoses or shoot each other dead in turf wars in the inner cities are best imprisoned for six hundred years or given a lethal injection in front of glad, vengeful witnesses on the orders of Governor Bush.

Governor Bush is a winner, you see, and the one hundred and fifty-two people he ordered killed (one a woman, the first Texas woman executed in a hundred years) were losers. And that's the way the divinity ordained it, we can't do a dang thing about it, just give the gosh-darn order to execute.

Winners got there, the myth continues, by hard work. They worked through the night in their twenties and so made their first million through hard, relentless, disciplined labour.

Even George Bush, the layabout, coke-sniffing, college-flunking, boozy, womanising grandson of Old Money, got there by hard work.

And Ted Turner, who inherited millions. And Rupert Murdoch, who inherited a newspaper.

It was hard work, and not family wealth, that made them winners.

And it was laziness, not family poverty, which made the other two hundred and five million Americans losers.

That's the explanation, and we're sticking to it.

115

This argument would be persuasive if there were not a whole lot fewer losers in other societies.

Though 2.2 million Americans are in gaol in any year, only five thousand nine hundred Swedes are. If Sweden were the same size as America this would be one hundred and ninety-eight thousand, less than a tenth of the number in American gaols.

And the number of murders (a sure sign of losers protesting their fates) per year in Britain is seven hundred and thirty-seven, compared with sixteen thousand in America.

Obesity, divorce, school shootings and appearances on *The Jerry Springer Show* in America outscore all other societies on earth.

So is it being born a loser, or being an American citizen, that is the main, predominant factor in stuffing up one's life?

Are Americans genetically stupider? Is that the reason?

Or is it the way they are treated?

116

Nelson Mandela looked like a loser for a while. He was in prison for twenty-seven years, derided as a terrorist, and many western conservative politicians – Soames, Thatcher, Wallace – wanted him hanged.

Muhammad Ali was a loser, big time, for a while. Stripped of his world heavyweight title for refusing to serve in Vietnam ('No Vietcong ever called me nigger') and, some say, for becoming a Black Muslim, he came back from oblivion to regain the world heavyweight crown and to light the Olympic torch in Atlanta as a national hero.

Winston Churchill was a loser big time, for many, many years. He lost Gallipoli, stuffed up the Gold Standard and (or so some say) caused the World Depression, became an alcoholic and was a ridiculed back-bench has-been for ten years, and Robert Rhodes James's book *Churchill: A Study in Failure 1900–1939* reflected this.

But each of them came back from their various purgatories – as did George W. Bush from alcoholism, drug abuse and repeated failure in oil-drilling, baseball management and congressional politics. And it looks, from these examples, as if 'loser' is not a useful concept in economic prediction for individuals.

And the Ronald Reagan slogan of 'backing winners' is not a helpful one.

Ken Lay of Enron was a winner, two hundred and fifty million a year at age fifty-eight. And he ended having a heart attack at age sixty-four after he was convicted and faced a likelihood of thirty years in gaol for cooking the figures.

Donald Rumsfeld was a winner, the only man twice appointed Secretary of Defense, and is now the most execrated politician – an incompetent, unindicted mass murderer and impelled mastermind of torture – since Richard Nixon. He was a winner till he was seventy-four.

And look at him now.

117

Losers, though, in America are comprehensively punished for losing.

They have their unemployment benefits taken away from them. They have their babies taken away from them.

If they are busted three times for stealing pizzas (three strikes and you're out), they get twenty-five years in gaol.

If they go to gaol in Florida, Alabama, Kentucky, Virginia, Arizona, Delaware, Maryland, Mississippi, Nevada, Tennessee, Washington or Wyoming, they can lose the *right to vote for the rest of their lives.*

An estimated 5.3 million Americans, most of them black, have been disfranchised in this way.

(Republicans stay in power in these states by gaoling enough blacks for minor felonies – drug abuse and burglary – and taking their votes away from them.)

118

Economic fundamentalism also comes after losers, killing great numbers of them, through the workings, in America, of its 'health system' (your money or your life).

Eighteen thousand US citizens who have no health cover die each year because of this.

But many, many more *with* health cover die too because of exclusionary clauses in their various health plans.

People with 'pre-existing' conditions are judged ineligible, when they grow sick, for any health care whatever, *regardless of the amount of money they have paid in premiums up to that point.*

Among these pre-existing conditions, according to Michael Moore's remarkable documentary *Sicko*, are Addison's disease, adrenal disorder, adult respiratory distress syndrome, AIDS, ARC or HIV, alcohol dependence, Alport's syndrome, Alzheimer's disease, amyloidosis, amyotrophic lateral sclerosis, anemia, anencephaly, aneurysm, angina, angioplasty, ankylosing spondylitis, anticoagulant therapy, aortic arch arteritis, aortic sufficiency / stenosis / regurgitation, aortitis, Arnold-Chiari malformation, arterial embolism (clot), arterial occlusion, arteriosclerosis, atherosclerosis, arteriosclerosis obliterans (ASO), arteriovenous malformation, arteritis, artificial heart valve, Asperger's syndrome, ascites, ataxia telangiectasia, atherosclerosis obliterans, atherosclerosis thrombotic disease, arterial fibrillation, atrial septal defect and autism.

And these are just the As.

Any treatment paid for by the health fund is regarded by its auditors as a 'loss' and any treatment *not* paid for a pleasing outcome.

In the documentary, a woman is told that treatment for her brain tumour is 'non-threatening' and therefore can't be paid for, and she dies of it anyway.

Another young woman with cervical cancer at twenty-two is told she is 'too young' to have this cancer and refused *for this reason* the thousands of dollars she needs to stop dying, pays it herself, and goes to Canada, where all diseases, regardless of their eccentricity or pre-existence or costliness, are free; or paid for in taxes by everyone.

In a moving sequence a young mother with *full cover* and an eighteen-month-old daughter took her by ambulance to the nearest hospital with a temperature of more than a hundred and four. The hospital checked and said her health fund, Kaiser Permanente, would not pay for the tests and the antibiotics *in that hospital*. She had to go to a Kaiser-owned hospital.

She wouldn't do this, and begged the hospital she was in, Martin Luther King, to take and treat her little daughter. They kept refusing. Her daughter had a seizure. She cried and begged, and they dragged her out of the hospital. Hours passed before she got the little girl to the Kaiser hospital, but she went into cardiac arrest.

'They worked on her for thirty minutes,' she says in the film, 'trying to revive her. And the doctors came in and let us know that she had expired. I was in a daze, a real daze. It just didn't seem real. I just held her. I held her and I told her that Mommy tried her best to help her, to make sure that she was going to get the treatment she needed to receive. And that I was sorry I wasn't able to help her.'

119

One might ask if it was wrong for economic rationalism (as we used to call it) to kill that little girl, or whether it would have been better if she had grown up and got a job and had children and paid taxes.

Not so, apparently. There was no alternative.

The system was working and it's the best economic system there has ever been.

And losers deserve every punishment they get.

120

In Barack Obama's memoir *Dreams from My Father* are a number of losers, all blood relatives of his.

His brother David, who was killed while racing on a motorbike to get his older brother Roy's papers and bring them back to the police station where he was under arrest.

His brother Roy, who got into a fight in a nightclub over a woman and, being without his papers, caused his brother David's death and thereafter in drunkenness and womanising wasted his life.

His young brother Stephen who refuses to go to college, preferring to hang about Nairobi and mope.

His father Barack Obama Senior who keeps contradicting his teachers and getting expelled and, though Harvard educated, contradicts his Prime Minister Kenyatta so publicly he is denied a government job and falls to drunken womanising and death in a car accident after begetting numerous children by different women whom he ill-treats and abandons.

It is not too big a stretch of the bow-string to presume that Barack Obama, President of the United States, might have suffered a like fate if he had grown up uncertain and scared in Kenya among plaintive poor relations with a turbulent, violent, drunken father and not, as it turned out, relatively prosperous in Indonesia with a good Muslim education and a mother who got him up at four a.m. each morning to school him in grammatical English and American history.

It is not too big a pull at the bow-string to suggest he would be dead now in a knife-fight over a woman or in a road accident like his father and his brother and *this is the kind of fate you slam into in post-colonial countries where economic fundamentalism has bruised the souls of its people and forbidden them, as Empires in their aftermaths do, the audacity of hope.*

And if Empire – or as it is now called, Global Economics – is nasty enough to kill a Barack Obama in his adolescence or infancy, or send him into drunken womanising for thirty years, what good is it?

How does it justify itself?

By saying, 'Obamas are losers, and there's nothing you can do for them'.

'They are all no-hopers, look at their track record. They're losers. Forget them.'

Oh really?

121

In *Sicko* a woman doctor, long a risk-assessor of a health fund, says, 'I am here primarily today to make a public confession.

'In the spring of 1987, as a physician, I denied a man a necessary operation that would have saved his life, and thus caused his death. No person and no group has held me accountable for this, because in fact what I did was I saved a company half a million dollars for this.

'And, furthermore, this particular act secured my reputation as a good medical director, and it insured my continued advancement in the health-care field.

'I went from making a few hundred dollars a week as a medical reviewer to an escalating six-figure income as a physician executive. In all my work, I had one primary duty, and that was to use my medical expertise for the financial benefit of the organisation for which I worked. And I was told repeatedly that I was not denying care, I was simply denying payment.

'I know how managed care maims and kills patients, so I'm here to tell you about the dirty work of managed care. And I'm haunted by the thousands of pieces of paper on which I have written that deadly word "denied". Thank you.'

She spoke of course of losers, who are expendable, roadkill, people an efficient system doesn't need.

And murders therefore.

122

In proof of the *inefficiency* of the American health system Sweden's average life span is two and a half years longer than America's; or, if you don't believe that, Canada's average life span, because of free health care, is three years longer than America's, and the *poorest* Briton lives two years longer on average than the *richest* American.

And Americans pay on average three thousand and seventy-four dollars *more* than the average payment in the industrialised world of two thousand one hundred and ninety-three dollars per person, that is, twice as much in any year.

For pills that can cost a hundred and fourteen dollars a bottle.

For surgery that can cost four hundred and fifty thousand dollars and force you to sell your house.

Or stays in hospital that can be forty-eight thousand dollars a week as opposed to nothing in Canada, Britain and France.

There is no alternative.

Or, as highway robbers used to say, *Your money or your life.*

123

The Americans who die three years before Canadians cost their economy each year, probably, five billion dollars in goods unbought, holidays not taken and taxes not paid.

This is one of the benefits *to the economy* of the free health system like Sweden's or Britain's.

You live to buy more things; discuss.

124

The idea that 'the user pays' when disease strikes and death looms is like saying to the families of the dead on 9/11, 'Don't come whingeing round this office, madam. If your husband was fool enough to put himself in that sort of danger on that plane at that hour, he deserves everything he got. And so do you for marrying him.'

'But – but – but,' she says, 'I couldn't *predict* 9/11, and neither could he.'

'That's none of our concern, madam, good day.'

Is health care a human right?

Economic fundamentalism doesn't think so.

It thinks you should pay through the nose for it.

Your money or your life.

125

In Africa, for instance, AIDS drugs are sold for three hundred and fifty dollars for a year's supply to families that earn two hundred dollars a year.

Though these drugs are free, or cost ten dollars, in England, and five cents in Cuba, in Botswana, where economic fundamentalism has its many adherents, AIDS-stricken children are allowed to die painful deaths at nine because of American companies' 'intellectual property' claims on these drugs, for which they charge 'the market price'.

Your money or your life.

Economic fundamentalism kills people; discuss.

No; amend that. It murders people.

In their hundreds of thousands.

Prove that I lie.

126

During the writing of this book, the condition of Stephen Hawking deteriorated and he was rushed to hospital.

He is now sixty-seven.

The British National Health Service has kept him alive and intellectually functional for thirty-eight years. During that time, he has altered the way we see the universe.

The American health system, had he lived there, would have disqualified him from treatment unless he put up big money (your money or your life) in millions of dollars, and lacking that sort of money, he would have died twenty years ago; discuss.

There would have been no alternative.

127

Should we stop talking about death for a while?

Yes, let's do that, I think.

Let's talk about its close accomplice, money.

THE EVIDENCE OF
THINGS NOT SEEN

128

In my previous book I wrote of Picasso's lightning sketches in bars and cafes.

He would go sometimes to a particular bar where poor bohemian friends would eat and drink.

Sometimes they didn't have money to pay the bill. And Picasso would do a lightning sketch of one of them, or the waiter, on the back of the bill, and sign it, and not so much the sketch but *the signature* was assessed by the restaurant owner to be of sufficient worth to equal or surpass the owed amount. It became currency.

It became a substitute for money.

129

And this is how it is sometimes. Things that did not exist a moment before are thought, however insubstantial, to be worth money.

A busker's song. A speech by a fundamentalist preacher in a wooden church when the collection is taken up. A performance by the Rolling Stones of songs already available on their CDs in a big sports stadium. A one-man show of Kenneth Branagh reciting Shakespeare at lunchtime in a London pub. A kind of magic attaches to a moment in time for which a witness pays eighty, ninety, two hundred dollars.

A similar magic, a similar aura, somehow clings to a red dress worn by Vivien Leigh in *Gone with the Wind* when sold at auction. An original, unreleased tape of John Lennon singing. A lock of Marilyn Monroe's dyed blonde hair. The life-mask of Abraham Lincoln. The foot moulds of John F. Kennedy's feet, whose slight deformity meant he wore hand-crafted shoes.

130

In the Middle Ages, splinters of the True Cross were likewise thought to have magical value, and price-negotiations occurred. The Turin Shroud, apparently stained by Christ's death-image, people queued and paid for centuries to see. As they did for the corpse, in Cairo Museum, of Ramses II, a person mentioned in the Bible. And Jesus' alleged tomb, in which a priest reads mass with a microphone in Jerusalem.

These connections of religious awe and proffered money are particularly notable in the world of art. More than Leonardo da Vinci earned in a lifetime is paid in a couple of weeks by tourists gazing at his unremarkable small green painting the Mona Lisa. Van Gogh's indifferent portrait of Dr Gachet lately sold for 82.5 million dollars. One of Francis Bacon's Popes went for 26.6 million pounds. And a print of Andy Warhol's Campbell's Soup can, based heavily on what Campbell's Soup cans really look like, still sells, though there are thousands of them, for a hundred and twenty dollars.

Who decides the worth of these things?

A mood, a rumour, a headline, a scandal, a murder apparently changes the value. JFK memorabilia went up in price when he was murdered. Shavings from Elvis Presley's sideburns skyrocketed when he died.

A kind of worshipful valuation occurs; a vulgar struggle between millionaires, a well-timed auction at Sotheby's. Alan Bond, widely thought to be a bit of a philistine, paid 53.9 million dollars for Van Gogh's *Irises*, the first time such a sum for a painting had been offered or accepted, and the mania built from there.

A sketchbook from Yves Saint Laurent now commands forty thousand dollars. A Bob Dylan mouth organ ten thousand.

131

Now and then a forgery turns up. A Rembrandt self-portrait, a shimmering Van Gogh field of wheat is proved, or said, to be by another hand. And its value plummets, though it's equally well painted, and exquisitely composed.

But it has lost its *mana*, its connection with a dead deity. And its image has been blasphemed.

The connection between art and religion, always there in ancient times, continues.

132

Two big questions arise from this. What is value? And what is money?

It's worth asking what value is because the Economic Meltdown of 2008 occurred when houses said to be worth eighty thousand dollars ended up selling for five thousand dollars or, in one case, one dollar.

133

Money, though, is something else again.

Till 1933 the US dollar was redeemable in gold, a yellow heavy metal thought beautiful if useless in many sun-reverencing ancient cultures. After 1933 it was just paper.

Paper, plus the *faith* people had in it.

('Money is the substance of things hoped for,' St Paul might have said, 'the evidence of things not seen.')

Yet people slave for fifty years to pile it up. They risk their lives to rob banks of it. They hide it in mattresses and hatbands and shoes. They reverence it as they would a splinter of the True Cross.

Where Barack Obama's grandfather paid fifteen cows for the virginity of his grandmother, Edward VIII, in about the same year, paid with the throne of England for the shopsoiled vagina of Wallis Simpson and Mickey Rooney four years later paid cash for Ava Gardner, in a 'prenuptial agreement', signed in the event of a marriage break-up, of half a million dollars.

Paper money had come of age. Though its value in gold was no longer guaranteed, the Federal Reserve Bank reckoned it was okay and Ava's virginity was Mickey's for the taking and 'in an all-night sexual symphony', according to her biographer, Lee Server, he took it. He had paid good greenbacks for it.

Why a virgin is so prized and a seasoned, practised, loving woman of, say, twenty-three not preferred has never been established.

Male pride, I guess.

Or, as Baron von Blixen-Finecke in the film *Out of Africa* said, 'I have to marry a virgin. I can't stand criticism.'

134

What, though, is the process by which the greenback, the American dollar, gains and keeps its value?

By a certain fraudulent stealth, we're told.

It comes off a *printing press* that the Federal Reserve Bank, the Fed, sets going from time to time, and it's *loaned out at interest*, the rate of interest varying, sometimes one percent, sometimes five, sometimes nine, to other banks, which lend it out at a greater rate of interest, sometimes ten, sometimes eleven, to, say, fools who want to buy in Michigan houses whose prices may fall to a dollar if things go bad.

If you look at this arrangement carefully, you will find a flaw in it.

Because the money is loaned by the Fed to the banks at interest, and it must be paid back, and all the money there is comes off the Fed's printing presses, there's never enough money in circulation to pay back the debt.

So though the money turns over, from subprime mortgage to pension fund to hedge fund to insurance of that hedge fund, though it moves around the economy and around the world, the full amount is never there.

It has to be imagined.

Like the value of the eighty-thousand-dollar Michigan house that sold for a dollar.

Or like God's love.

Or it has to be borrowed from the Chinese, who want to be paid in greenbacks too, and there just aren't enough of them. And there never can be.

Under capitalism, we are always short of the money that makes capitalism make sense.

Which it doesn't.

135

The Fed can print more, of course, and leave it in buckets round the supermarkets, but this is very dangerous as recent cash-printings in Zimbabwe lavishly, foolishly proved.

136

In Zimbabwe the Prime Minister is printing a lot of money.

This is because the price of a loaf of bread went from two hundred Zimbabwe dollars in 2006 to one hundred thousand in 2007 to 1.6 trillion in 2008.

And this in turn was because the country's Prime Minister, Robert Mugabe, was held to be a tyrant and a madman by the 'civilised world', which put embargoes on trading with him.

His principal sin was to have driven white farmers, killing some of them, off land their forefathers had seized in the late nineteenth century – illegally seized, we now would say, by British conquerors armed with rifles and machine guns back when the multi-tribal region was called 'Rhodesia'. His lesser sins were to give it to men who farmed it incompetently, and to rig elections and beat up rival politicians impertinent enough to stand against him, and sometimes kill their followers.

A hero of Black Africa in 1980 when he won the Prime Ministership in a fair, democratically fought election, he had become by 2008, at the age of eighty-four, a stubborn, rancorous embarrassment. Though other leaders who had long admired him had begged him to go quietly, he wouldn't – or maybe his criminalised army, who did his murdering for him, wouldn't let him go.

This led to banknote inflation as preposterous as that of Weimar Germany, where a retired civil servant's life savings might go in a wheelbarrow to a grocery store and purchase only two days' food.

And largely because of the inflation, and the lack of saleable foreign goods, unemployment hit ninety-four percent.

137

Could this happen to the USA?

Well . . . America now owes China 1.25 trillion dollars, and China cheerfully banks the forty billion dollars in interest it first lends America to pay itself with each year, and it's thought that by 2030 the sum owed will be three trillion and the annual interest the US pays will be one hundred and thirty billion; this is more than the total budget of Botswana.

At this point, it has been postulated, or in 2020 or 2015 or 2012, China might find the greenback unappealing – as the 'civilised world' has the Zimbabwe dollar – and ask to be paid in euros. Or Swiss francs. Or Japanese yen.

This will send the greenback into free-fall, and America into fifty percent unemployment, and turn it into the Mexico of Canada. And it is hoped that China won't do this.

138

But China's memories are long, and its leaders are aware that America once killed nine hundred thousand of its people in a war in Korea that is not, as yet, officially ended.

And they may call up the loan, or ask for, say, Alaska as part-payment of it. Or California.

This is the fix George W. Bush got America into.

It's worth enquiring how this happened.

HE TRIED TO KILL MY DAD

139

George W. Bush correctly suspected that his father thought him a moron.

He sought to redress this by finishing what his father failed to do in Iraq.

This, and it was the costliest Oedipal purge in world history, was to unseat Saddam Hussein. Saddam had plotted the assassination with a bomb of George and Barbara Bush on a bridge in Saudi Arabia in 1994. 'After all, this is the guy who tried to kill my dad,' the President said winningly, in justification of bombing a country to smithereens.

Much as Churchill and Eisenhower in 1953, on hearing Hitler was alive and living in Argentina, would have bombed that country to smithereens.

Serve the Argies right, George W. Bush would have said.

140

There was more to it than this, of course.

George W. Bush had failed in the oil business and Iraq

had at least seventy-eight billion barrels of oil. Once it was 'privatised' American co-owners of it would make a lot of money, and some of it (possibly) trickle back to his company Arbusto Energy.

'Arbusto' is Spanish for 'Bush'.

His Vice President Dick Cheney, moreover, had been for five years CEO (on 8.8 million a year on average, or one thousand and four dollars fifty-seven cents an hour) of Halliburton, a company that liked to rebuild war-smashed countries and deliver precooked hamburgers to hungry armies and be paid in billions by the US government to do so.

'Socialism for the deserving rich,' as Gore Vidal once said of the US system, 'and free enterprise for the undeserving poor.'

141

So George Bush went to war, though the UN said he couldn't and Colin Powell, his own Secretary of State, said he shouldn't, and Tony Blair wished he wouldn't.

He alleged Saddam had atomic bombs and things he could chuck at Israel, or was thinking of getting some, though Hans Blix said he wasn't, or hadn't yet proved to be doing so.

He thought the war would 'pay for itself' once the oil started flowing, and Halliburton rebuilding cities he'd thoughtfully bombed to bits to help Dick's bottom line (though no longer CEO he was a major shareholder; this was the American way), and three hundred thousand troops had subdued twenty-six million Muslim Iraqis, unaccountably annoyed that thirty-one Christian countries had invaded them and were hauling random groups of them off the street and torturing them in Abu Ghraib. There were ninety-four Iraqis for every invading soldier, none of them very happy, but this didn't daunt George Bush who was assured his gigantic Humvees and helicopter-gunships (and the oil revenue of course) were all that were needed to win their hearts and minds.

At this point, knowing the war would cost very little (he asked at first only sixty billion dollars to wage it), George Bush decided to bring America's taxes down.

142

This was the first time any leader had done this in world history. What you usually do when you go to war is put taxes up to *pay* for the war.

And the taxes came down for corporate America, and the CEOs' wages went up – to, oh, five thousand dollars an hour, day and night, on average, including weekends. Or something of that order.

It was the 'backing winners' policy of Ronald Reagan, whom George Bush admired, and in his public persona pretty much imitated.

And George Bush, who had inherited from Bill Clinton

a one-hundred-and-twenty-seven-billion-dollar *surplus*, had delivered by 2005 a four-hundred-billion-dollar *deficit* (by spending four hundred and forty billion on a war he refused to pay for) and by January 2009, when he left office, a deficit of one trillion dollars, in part to pay for the meltdown bail-out, a meltdown he'd helped cause with six years of unfunded war-making in two foreign countries.

143

George W. felt taxes shouldn't be paid by those who spent them, by the big corporations like Lockheed Martin who got two hundred billion of taxpayers' money in 2001, less after that, to build Humvees and fighter bombers and UAVs – the unmanned drones armed with Hellfire missiles that shot up random Pakistanis in illegal airstrikes – and, of course, the rockets involved in Star Wars.

144

Star Wars was a bright idea of Ronald Reagan who saw kids playing Space Invaders in a milk bar once and said aha and zowie.

Officially called the Strategic Defense Initiative (SDI), its plan was to put rockets in satellites, and when the bad guys fired intercontinental nuclear rockets at the United States, to shoot them down *from outer space.*

Though some experts said this was like 'aiming a speeding bullet at another speeding bullet' and was very likely to universally fail, and other experts wondered what country, precisely, would attack America in this way, and why, if the weapons worked, they would try to attack it in this way, knowing they wouldn't succeed and would themselves be H-bombed back to the Stone Age in consequence of their lunacy a few minutes later.

But it was Ronald Reagan's pet idea, and it went ahead.

And, though it still isn't working, it consumes about two hundred and twenty-eight dollars from each US household per year for Lockheed Martin alone; about twenty-seven billion in all, for Lockheed alone, every year.

This is enough to sustain four thousand small theatre companies for a thousand years on the interest alone.

Or, probably, cure cancer.

145

The Bush Era proved, though, that a new kind of war could be waged very cheaply, Star Wars notwithstanding, against America and her allies. This was the War on the Free Market of the Suicide Bombers.

146

Suicide bombers are cheap to breed, school, inspire and motivate and relatively cheap (the full explosive garment probably costs two hundred and twenty dollars) to arm and point at strategic targets.

They are not only 'the smartest bomb there is' but, in

proportion to the effect they have, the cheapest, most 'efficient' weapon there is.

Less than forty of them in various restaurants and marketplaces obliterated, pretty much, Israel's tourist economy, and another twelve in slow-moving traffic with Kalashnikovs ended forever Test cricket in Pakistan and the millions of tourist dollars that sport provided.

Nineteen more (perhaps the figure was larger if one adds the basement explosions in the Towers and the Pentagon) brought the world's largest economy to a standstill on 9/11, cancelling all flights and shaming the FBI, the Air Force and the Presidency, and starting an endless, fruitless, wasteful War on Terror that has cost eight hundred and fifty-two billion thus far, while provoking derision for America worldwide and helping hobble its economy.

All this, in Israel, Pakistan and the US, was achieved by less than a hundred earnest young men and their impelled Muslim tutors and mentors, perhaps two hundred more, with not a WMD or an ICBM or a fighter bomber in sight.

They learned the ideas of 'efficiency' and 'cost-effectiveness' and 'economic rationalism' from the corporate west and with them brought these formidable nations to their knees.

147

For how is one to deter a young man eager to die for his nation's honourable cause? How would you deter him?

You can shoot him before he gets to his intended crowded place but his brother or his cousin will replace him within a year or so, and there are twenty million others (probably) keen to do similar work and procreating children of similar belief.

How does the free market sort this out?

It can't.

When death by angry bomb-triggering suicide is a part of the accounting all neo-liberal economic theory goes to hell.

Willing death wipes out the numbers on any ledger; discuss.

Willing death is a black hole that sucks up all the numbers; discuss.

148

Economic fundamentalist, free-market methods are also used by the pirates of Somalia.

Like economic rationalists they despise regulation and go where weaker players fear to go. They target a vulnerable entity, as United Fruit did Guatemala and George Bush Iraq, and with violence change its command-structure, and then demand bags of money in return for not destroying it altogether.

As I write these words, four ships off the Horn of Africa are under the command of pirates, who by 'disproportionate warfare' are humiliating America again.

They attacked the seventeen-thousand-tonne vessel *Maersk Alabama*, and after an exchange of gunfire kidnapped Captain Richard Phillips and took him away in their small boat as a hostage. In the gunfight the Americans captured a pirate, and proposed to give him back in exchange for the captain. But the pirates reneged on the deal, got their own man back, sank their own boat, and now hold Captain Phillips in a lifeboat.

US battleships are heading towards Somalian waters and Hillary Clinton is 'monitoring the situation'.

It's a dwarfed form of imperialism, or asset-stripping, or company takeover, and the pirates seem to be enjoying it.

Are they free marketeers like any other, using their economic strengths against the cowering vulnerable, or are they in breach of some kind of moral law?

If they are, who else is? And what does it say?

That you shouldn't threaten people in return for advantage?

Really?

149

But this is what economic fundamentalists do every day. They sell for instance to Israel those cluster-bombs whose tiny progeny, known as 'bomblets', lie around on farmlands for decades and blow up frolicking children. They sell them for about thirteen thousand dollars each, knowing that Israel has war-criminal tendencies, and they do not flinch from selling them on any philosophical ground.

How are they different morally from the pirates of the Gulf of Suez or the suicide bombers of Gaza? They kill at random, or threaten with death at random, people who mean no harm and gain advantage, monetary or political, for having done so.

It's no wonder capitalists talk of 'making a killing'.

Killing is one of the things they do best.

And selling the means of killing.

It's not a level playing field, it's a killing field; discuss.

150

The guilt of arms traders has been with us ever since Alfred Nobel, who invented dynamite, gave us in expiation of his own growing war guilt the Nobel Peace Prize, but it doesn't seem to affect the business practice of certain CEOs in England and America.

Manufacturing weapons of destruction is a great British industry, one of the biggest in the world.

Occasionally eminent people take umbrage at this. Princess Diana was one, but a convenient accident removed her from the equation and her prime foe BAE Systems continued to manufacture fighter jets and mortars and sell them to, say, Libya, Saudi Arabia, Israel and Pakistan.

Discuss.

LITTLE WHITE FLOWERS THAT GROW IN THE BRAIN

151

Is there any mercy, one might wonder, in the system? Or *potential mercy*?

Is there a way, as the former Australian Leader of the Opposition Mark Latham once suggested, of 'civilising global capital'? (Or, as I paraphrased it, 'house-training the crocodile'?) Any way to persuade or bully or legislatively force it into economic good manners, civic responsibility, the ordinary humanism that most of us in the mort-gaged, bill-paying, child-rearing, college-going classes subscribe to?

152

Well, let's run a scenario. Let's do a hypothetical. Let's have a hypothesis.

Let's imagine it becomes known that mobile phones cause brain cancer, or serious nerve damage, or memory loss, or attention deficit disorder (ADD).

Which they probably do. One or other of them, they do.

What would global capitalism do in such a case?

How would it respond?

153

For global capitalism, in such a case, would be in a bit of a fix. A good deal of its business relies now on swift contact, on transmitted SMSs, on broadcast phone images – from, for instance, the floor of the stock exchange, or a war zone, or a plane crash site, or a troubled meeting in a Tokyo office, or a yacht at sea.

What will global capitalism do?

154

It will do, I think, what it did in the 1950s with cigarettes. It will commission tests, and the tests will show that though *some* correlation between 'excessive mobile phone use' and mobile-phone-shaped cancers *seemingly* exists, this happens, as it turns out, more to children and older people, and its biggest customer base, young adults, need not worry too much yet.

Has this indeed happened? Has it happened in fact, in recent history?

Oh yes.

155

Global capitalism, in short, when threatened at its heart, its irreducible core, will react as the tobacco industry and the asbestos industry did in the 1950s, '60s, '70s, '80s and '90s.

With big, engulfing cover-ups.

Even when the product is one whose rays (when you call, say, London from Sydney) can penetrate heavy layers of concrete, travel to the nearest phone tower, then on to a relay station, up to a satellite twenty-two thousand miles out in space, piercing clouds that can throw into turbulence jumbo jets, then, reversing the procedure, come all the way back to an organ an inch away from your frontal cortex, *it will do that organ no harm.*

Or very little harm if you are over sixteen and under sixty-three.

Let's face it, mobile phones *do* do harm.

It's a no-brainer.

And would it be better for the overall health, if not necessarily the economic health, of humankind to ban them outright?

Oh yes.

Has this happened?

No.

Is global capitalism, then, currently behaving as it usually does, covering up the harm it does and killing people in their scores of millions to improve the bottom line?

Looks like it.

156

The Somalian pirates have all been killed and Captain Richard Phillips rescued by a series of shrewd manoeuvres and superior gunpower.

The incident is being hailed as President Obama's first foreign policy victory. He showed nerves of steel apparently, in ordering the rescue, and so did Captain Phillips, in the water and under fire.

And so, for a day or two, a few more watery miles of trade route have been preserved.

Let us give thanks for that, and continue to talk of global capitalism, more nervously perhaps.

157

While writing this chapter the author discovered that studies of early childhood had proved that a baby aged six months hungers to be taught language, and babies who do not have a loved person talking to them tenderly at that age grow up stupider, more sociopathic and frigid. That mothers, or grandmothers, or attentive family members talking to a baby round the clock are essential for normal intelligence in a child to be achieved, and a babysitter, or an early-age kindergarten, does not provide this.

This means capitalism, whose house prices and rents mean mothers must work, is breeding – has bred – a generation of losers: drink-prone, violence-prone,

divorce-prone, ill-read, incommunicative and cantanker-
ous. You meet them every day.

Well done, capitalism. You know it makes sense to treat
babies this way.

There is no alternative.

158

It kills babies too, or so I'm told.

Let us look at the case of Xuan Le (not her real name),
a determined young Chinese woman who escaped from
China and while in detention as an illegal immigrant in
Australia had a baby, and then proposed gamely to have
another baby. *Don't do it*, the detention officials said. A second child is illegal in China and we're probably sending
you back.

Ignoring these warnings, she became pregnant again,
and, sure enough, five months in, they proposed to send
her back.

She begged them to relent, saying the Chinese would
hold her down and abort her; to relent at least for as long
as it took for her baby to be born, after which she could
seek entry to another country. A public campaign was
started up in the media to let her stay.

But the Australian government, run by John Howard,
feared that if she was let stay on these grounds, two
hundred million other Chinese women, and their two
hundred million husbands, might seek to come in for the

same reason, with their two hundred million growing foetuses.

So they sent her back.

And she was arrested by the Chinese and aborted in her ninth month.

There was no alternative.

Global economics is a licence to kill; discuss.

And capitalism involves a lot of killing; discuss.

And it never *had* a human face.

WORK IN THE OLD
HOME TOWN

159

We have seen thus far that capitalism overpays its CEOs, it scares and starves its workers, it kills lots of people and doesn't care who it kills. It also manufactures *as a preference* all sorts of weapons and sells them to people who kill each other. It props up with these weapons those murderous regimes that buy them. It is indifferent to what would seem a fundamental error in its calculations, that with tobacco and bad water and over-expensive AIDS drugs and mobile phones it kills its customers, and, when sacking them, loses by the 'multiplier effect' millions more of them each year, and by the poverty it achieves (and exploits) by these means it provokes those pirates and suicide bombers and communist and neo-communist regimes which, in the Middle East and Africa and Asia and the former USSR and South America, may prove to be its undoing.

It seems curiously optimistic about its future and, like America, unrepentant of the deeds that got it into this almighty fix, and keen in the face of the subprime meltdown to create even more poverty, and enemies, and terrorists and pirates and 'rogue regimes' with clout like Venezuela and Russia and thus secure its own extinction.

You have to admire its cunning sometimes, though.

Sometimes it makes money by giving it away.

To Israel, for instance.

160

The US gives Israel three billion a year and with it Israel buys weapons for its 'beleaguered' army, navy and air force, the long-range rockets and helicopter-gunships and mortar-firing battleships with which it lately pulverised Gaza, killing three hundred children, and causing the deaths of hundreds more through the usual means of bad water, electricity outages, dead babies in blacked-out humidicribs, the arbitrary arrest of breadwinners, the 'targeted' assassination of Cabinet ministers and propaganda suggesting they had no choice (there is no alternative) in the face of rockets fired at a couple of towns that had killed, in the last five years, fewer people than America's backyard swimming pools.

These weapons anyhow showed up in the 'profits' columns of Lockheed Martin, Raytheon and Boeing though the US had *given* the money to its purchasers and *borrowed* the money from China, fourteen billion dollars a year at an interest rate of (on average) four percent, or five hundred and sixty million a year, which it then gave to Israel to buy US war machines with.

And the US government, friends of Lockheed Martin, Raytheon and Boeing and those Halliburton-like entities that will now clean up and rebuild Gaza, has made damn sure no peace will erupt in Gaza, or the West Bank, by demonising the duly-elected party, Hamas, and refusing to deal with it, until it 'renounces violence'.

No such demand has been put on Israel, which does a whole lot of killing, because this might halt the continuing series of 'war incidents' that provokes those 'incursions' (a cuter name for killing raids) which not only use up the weapons that Lockheed Martin sells, but advertises them.

Though Israel is in danger of being had up for war crimes, especially those associated with its illegal use of phosphorus bombs (for illumination, apparently, in broad daylight) that eat up the skin of howling 'civilians' (a bland old word for 'human beings') and end in excruciating pain the lives of a lot of children, it is likely no 'roadmap' will occur and the killing will continue and the sale, by Lockheed Martin, of weapons of mass destruction to Israel, which has a stash of atomic bombs and may use them soon if it gets any more irritated with the firecrackers falling harmlessly, mostly, and interrupting some Israelis' sleep.

So it all works together, you see, Lockheed Martin, Israel, foreign aid and endless war.

And China makes a whole lot of money.

Which is as it should be.

There is no alternative.

161

How China, a communist tyranny, got to be the dominant economic power of the twenty-first century is perhaps worth pondering.

After famines and persecutions that killed, oh, eighty million people it discovered a useful new method, called arithmetic.

If the majority of its billion people could be put to work, it decided, and its currency kept low, it could make a lot of things, and sell them to the rest of the world, more cheaply than the rest of the world could make them, and so cut out most of the competition.

In order to have eight hundred million people working it had to house and feed them which, being a socialist country, it was able to do by limiting the number of children each couple could have to one. Since most preferred a boy, many baby girls were murdered in their cribs. But, as the government had calculated, and rightly calculated (follow the arithmetic), the population inexorably came down. For every two old people who died, only one infant was born, or survived birth.

This brought down the amount of food that was required each year to feed the diligent workers.

These workers paid tiny rents, ate healthily and lived long lives and worked busily.

They made T-shirts and magnifying spectacles and radios and pocket calculators and paper shredders and microphones and biros and writing pads that sold all over the world, putting rival manufacturers out of business, at very low prices because the workers who made them paid very little rent, got almost free health care (seven dollars a year, mostly), had only one child to raise and asked for very low wages, and the *exchange rate was very low*; all these factors making possible the very low prices which wiped out, across the world, all significant competition.

Follow the arithmetic.

It's not very hard.

All this happened because China was a Command Economy.

This meant all its banks, and the money they printed and lent, were *regulated* by the government, which also set the exchange rate.

Economic fundamentalism argues that Command Economies never work.

That regulation stifles enterprise.

That currency should 'float'.

And economic fundamentalism, American style, now owes the Command Economy, Chinese style, one trillion two hundred and twenty-four billion dollars (a fairly accurate estimate, I would submit, of a figure China keeps secret) – plus, since you started reading this chapter, four hundred and sixty-five thousand five hundred and seventy-five dollars more in interest, or a number pretty close to that.

By 2030 it will owe 3.5 trillion dollars, or a number pretty close to that, twice that figure if its current wars go badly.

And economic fundamentalism works where communism fails; discuss.

This is a further Capitalist Delusion.

That the arithmetic works its way, and it has a future.

Even though Chinese communism, each year, has fewer mouths to feed; discuss.

And every citizen of America, a rich country, has in effect borrowed four thousand dollars in the last ten years from someone in China, a poor country; discuss.

Which is the rich country and which is the poor country?

Is a puzzlement, as Yul Brynner used to say.

162

One would have thought that Capitalism, when thus attacked by Communism, would have defended itself.

By, say, noting that China with its undervalued currency was cheating, and refusing to trade with it, refusing to buy its goods, until . . .

But this would mean protectionism, and economic fundamentalism doesn't believe in that.

It doesn't believe in it with an almost religious fervour.

163

Protectionism is not too hard a concept to understand, being pretty much what it sounds like.

You protect your own products by putting a tax on products that come in from overseas.

On a cowboy hat made by child slaves in Mumbai you put a one hundred percent import tax, thus ensuring the cowboy-hat-making industry in your country survives, and the people working in it keep their jobs, and spend their salaries on other things in the marketplace.

The 'protect' part of protectionism is about protecting jobs.

Economic fundamentalism thinks this is wrong, and no job should be protected anywhere.

(Except, in emergencies, the jobs of the senior executives of AIG and Goldman Sachs and so on, these are deserving cases. For them we break the rules.)

164

Protectionism has been with us for about five thousand years. Merchants crossing borders had to pay a tax, or bribe an official, to bring in silk, pearls, golden amulets, exotic textiles, spears, bows, frankincense, rock salt, monkeys, myrrh. This tax meant local goods were cheaper (if often inferior) when locally sold, a marketing practice one might call, I suppose, a Tilted Playing Field (TPF).

Much smuggling resulted from this, much piracy and

highway robbery, and diamonds concealed in the anuses of fugitive Jews in the years that followed the Spanish Persecution, the Massacre at York, the pogroms in Russia and Poland, and so on.

There were many breaches of border security, many illegal immigrants smuggling precious gifts.

But . . . it was a fairly good and stable system, as its longevity shows. Goods sold at the village market maintained their value. Eggs, fish, geese, pigs, cows commanded prices that were predictable. Gold, though valued, did not alter much in price in a thousand years.

And jobs stayed home and commanded adequate wages.

In Australia, Kelvinator fridges, Qualcast mowers, Chesty Bond singlets, Berlei bras, Tooheys beer, Cottee's jams, Bushells tea, Mynor cordials, Aeroplane Jelly, Arnott's biscuits, Bega cheese, BHP steel, Akubra hats and Holden cars were made and sold here, and hands-on company managers tested the products, approved the advertising, hired the staff, faced down the workers during disputes, fired their employees when they had to, face to face.

And none of this would have happened if the products had not been protected – by a one hundred and ninety-two percent impost on foreign clothes, fifty-seven percent on foreign cars, sixty-eight percent on foreign textiles, and so on.

But it also meant there were similar import taxes on Australian goods when entering other countries – fifty-nine percent on Australian wool, seventy-seven percent on Australian sugar going into America, and so on. So it went.

And so it came to pass that various *trade pacts* were connived by various countries in the decades after 1960 – the US, Singapore and most remarkably the European Economic Community, whose initial name was the Common Market – that 'eased' the tariff barriers between rival countries, and you could buy, say, Swiss cheese, or Italian wine, or a Galway sweater at a price still higher but not very much higher, than the local product.

And then a line was crossed, and jobs began to go.

Clothing factories closed in many country towns. Japanese radios eliminated AWA and Bakelite from the market. Kelvinator was taken over by the Swedes. Arnott's, Bushells, Tooheys, Aeroplane Jelly, BHP and Cottee's were sold or moved their managements overseas. As with Qantas, it became clear to the new CEOs (twenty-five to fifty dollars a minute) that cheaper labour would make the same goods in Taiwan, or India, or Kurdistan.

Mitsubishi's Australian factory managers found this too, and assembly line after assembly line closed down in the major Australian cities, after various Commonwealth and state governments had given them buckets of money not to, and moved their operations overseas.

But . . . there were cheaper T-shirts for those who still had jobs. Good perfume. Cheaper Audis and BMWs. Cheaper champagne and French cheeses like you wouldn't believe. If the choice was between a cheaper T-shirt or a son in work, the answer was obvious. You picked the T-shirt every time.

165

Now, since the Meltdown, protectionism is being shyly mentioned again, as a way of getting people back in productive jobs and buying things again, planning families again and building houses. But Brown, Obama, Sarkozy, Merkel and Rudd are horrified by this possibility.

Protectionism? Never.

Never again.

It was such a stuff-up last time.

166

Was it?

No; it wasn't, really.

167

In the 1960s in Australia when there was a fifty-seven percent tariff on foreign cars and a one hundred and ninety-two percent tariff on foreign clothes, there were country towns with a lot of jobs in them.

In the author's home town of Lismore, for instance, you could work in the Lismore Cordials bottling factory, or in Alfa Knitwear or AGR's department store or 2LM Radio or Robb and Brown's joinery, or in the Harris bicycle shop, or in the Base Hospital. You could get a job for life in the Rural Bank or teach Latin at Lismore High. You could be a motorcycle cop or a breaker of horses or an owner of racing dogs. There was work ushering in three cinemas, the Vogue, the Star Court and the Vanity, or typing theses for students or manning the front desk at the Workers' Club. You might become a cub reporter for the *Northern Star* or a telegram boy for the General Post Office or wield a shovel for the Department of Main Roads. There was work painting signs (with customers' illustrated faces) above the shops or nude modelling at the Technical College. There was work at the Goonellabah Orphanage and the St Vincent's Old People's Home. There was work for lawyers and doctors and even advertising men, and their buxom secretaries. And for a girl I loved, Rita Norton, in the library.

And this was a town of only sixteen thousand people. You could live all your life there, and raise your parents' grandchildren half a mile away from the house you spent your childhood in. You could ride bikes for a day to distant waterfalls with friends and never be thought in danger of sexual predators or road accident. You called the lady next door 'auntie' and if you returned to an empty house you could knock on her door and she'd feed you.

And this was when the system *wasn't* working, back in the bad old days of protectionism, where you kept your job lifelong.

That system was terrible, the economic fundamentalists say, an obvious failure and we must never go back to it.

It's much, much better now.

With protectionism gone, it's much, much better now.

168

The country towns are emptying for want of work. There are no local soft-drink factories, knitwear factories, few joineries, jobbing typists, usherettes and almost no cinemas. There is 'no demand' for Latin, Australian-made TVs and radios, artistic sign-painters, home visits from doctors, dance-hall pianists, radio announcers, soft drinks and advertising men.

Many of the jobs are going overseas, many of the products coming in from Taiwan. The T-shirts are inferior and don't last long but hell, they're cheaper and that's what counts. Isn't that what counts?

And there's almost no protection any more.

What a victory *that* was.

And no jobs for life.

What a victory.

169

Listen hard to this, and listen keenly. It isn't too hard to understand.

Protectionism protects jobs. That's what it's there for.

And people who have jobs buy things. That's how it works.

That's how an economy works.

Follow the arithmetic.

If you cut back jobs *for any reason*, you lose customers, breed criminals and pay thirty thousand dollars a year to keep them in gaol. And the figures don't add up, except to CEOs who get paid fifty dollars a minute for sacking people and little else.

Thanks to free trade, unemployment in America is now twenty percent, twenty-four percent probably, if you count the people currently in gaol, because the experts *exclude* from the count those teenage job-seekers, and old-age job-seekers, who applied for a job two months ago and haven't found one since.

And back when there was protection, or more protection, and there were lots of little country towns with a variety of jobs for life, the figure was four percent.

Protection means what it says. Our standing army protects us from invasion. Our condoms protect us from AIDS. Our cops and social workers protect our kids from roving pederasts. Our diphtheria injections protect us from fatal disease.

And our tariffs protect us from economic invasion, economic disease.

No-one has yet suggested our army should let in whatever invaders swarm up our beaches or descend in parachutes on our major cities.

Yet economic fundamentalists demand our government let in foreign corporations that attack and destroy our home towns, and seize their brand names and move them overseas, and pay their CEOs five hundred and fifty dollars an hour for doing so.

170

It's been said free trade assists Third World countries. That they can sell goods on the world market as they couldn't before.

This may be so.

But if the people of fifty-three African countries can't afford AIDS drugs at market price, and AIDS is infecting fourteen percent of the people in some of those nations, the free market can't be said to be working very well.

Should the AIDS drugs cost less? Then the free market is not free, surely.

And if a child under five is dying every second (and this is the current figure), what good is it?

The main thing is to keep paying CEOs fifty dollars a minute, day and night, year round, and not daring to ask why.

WHAT I SAY GOES

So much of capitalism works on the Unexamined Confident Assertion (UCA) – that the Head of the Federal Reserve is intelligent; that the Secretary of Defense is wise; that Israel's Prime Minister is keen to avoid needless bloodshed; that the French President's desire for a frequently-photographed-nude pop star is a pleasing eccentricity; that Silvio Berlusconi is not a priapic buffoon; that Russell Crowe deserves five years in gaol for throwing a phone at a shrugging hotel clerk – that we don't know, or we don't really know, what the truth is any more.

We are told for instance that the intercontinental megamedia corporation that Rupert Murdoch runs is a shining example of 'free speech' or 'press freedom' or 'freedom of opinion', so much so that one of his commentators calls himself 'the no-spin zone'.

But if you look at things closely you will find that none of his sixty-four thousand media employees has any freedom at all.

If they put in print or broadcast any opinion other than those decided by him or Roger Ailes who runs Fox News, they will be immediately sacked and publicly jeered thereafter. These include the former editors of *The Times, The Australian* and the *Wall Street Journal* and so on.

None of his one hundred and eighty newspaper editors across the world differs with his views (though one in New Zealand was allowed for a time to advocate a vote for Helen Clark); these, in sum, are very curious views indeed. They include, in no particular order:

That the market is currently over-regulated and needs to be 'freed up' even more. That Bush's Iraq adventure will 'halve the price of oil'. That Gore in November 2000 was trying to 'steal the election'. That Gore was 'too cold and wooden' to be President. That Bill Clinton's concealment of sex with Monica Lewinsky was reason enough to remove him from the Presidency. That Teddy Kennedy should be tried for murder and Prince Charles put in the loony-bin. That the seventeen thousand young women whose breasts Murdoch exposed on page three of the London *Sun* suffered no serious harm in their subsequent lives. That Margaret Thatcher was the saviour of Britain and Neil Kinnock 'a Welsh windbag' feared by all decent Englishmen for his Stalinist views. That Gough Whitlam deserved to be sacked in 1975 for planning to buy back Australia's mineral wealth for four billion dollars borrowed from 'unconventional sources'. That Glenn Beck is a great American and Rush Limbaugh a 'respected commentator'.

That Barack Obama, moreover, is a radical Muslim fundamentalist; a radical Christian fundamentalist; a terrorist; an inexperienced naïf; a soiled and cunning Chicago machine politician; that he favours detailed sex education for kindergarten children before they learn to read; that he kissed a man in the back of a taxi; that his memoir *Dreams from My Father* was written by Bill Ayers, the unindicted Chicago terrorist; that he 'pals around' with terrorists; that he is a Marxist, a Chávez-style Socialist, a devious demagogue keen to 'redistribute wealth' to worthless crack-addicted inner-city Blacks. That Michelle Obama is 'unpatriotic'. That Zeituni Onyango, his aunt, should be gaoled and then deported. And so on.

Murdoch is the CEO of a big multinational corporation, News Limited, and is seventy-eight years old. It would be normal for his Board of Directors on hearing these views, and noting his age, to replace him with someone more informed and mentally acute. They would do this on the grounds that he might bring the corporation into disrepute, political derision and legal danger.

But capitalism doesn't work that way. It entrenches hubristic fools at the top of things until they blow themselves up. It is, in the end, and in most cases, highly inefficient.

172

But it was very good, for a time, at convincing you its purposes are moral, and its policies sane.

It convinced two billion people, for instance, that Iraq had 'weapons of mass destruction' that it would soon rain down on Israel when Iraq had none. What one might call the Confidently Asserted Untruth (the CAU) goes a long way with an undereducated audience, or an underinformed one (which is to say an American one) towards convincing them of what is being said: the early estimates on 9/11 of 'sixty thousand dead' in the crumbling towers; the repeated assertion that the Vietnam War was a 'noble cause', though it killed and maimed seven million people, won no hearts and minds and resulted, after our shameful defeat, in the rather nice little country we see now.

But it's no more true, of course, than the equally confident assertion that Scientology is the way back to self-esteem, or that angels are watching closely and weeping when we masturbate or drink Budweiser or fail to do our homework.

It is a CAU, that's all, and the principal weapon of the Capitalism Delusion.

And the unexamined confident assertion is quite often believed by the asserter, the CEO on four dollars a second, day and night, all year round, whose baffled underlings don't dare contradict him once he gets into his rhetorical stride.

It is certain, for instance, that Donald Rumsfeld believed that a 'lean and mean' invading force of two hundred and fifty thousand men and their megaweapons could subdue a nation of twenty-six million resentful, warlike people. *He heard himself say it so often* he knew it had to be right.

And so did Ken Lay at Enron. He knew *and simultaneously did not know* that his figures were cooked, and his company a billion dollars in hock. He had confidence, like most religious men, that the Invisible Hand would shake things down somehow, shake them down his way.

And so did the fools of AIG when they awarded themselves their million-dollar bonus moneys out of government bail-out funds made necessary by their incompetence.

This eerie confidence, this self-delusion, is common in capitalism and its kissing cousin, Italian fascism. Il Duce decides his high-strutting, chin-thrusting policy of world conquest, and his underlings dare not tell him that his tanks break down a lot and his soldiers would rather be home with their wives.

173

And thus it is in the matter of tariff protection.

174

In 1916 and 1917 General Haig, a close relative of several Scottish CEOs (they made their fortune in whisky) knew, and knew for certain, that 'one more big push' was all that was required to rout the stubborn Germans from their trenches and send them running back to the Motherland and a meek surrender would follow. He just knew it.

And he tried the big push; and again; and again. He tried it with tanks, a new weapon. He tried it with mustard gas, which the wind blew back over his own troops, blinding some and damaging many lungs.

And he tried the big push again. It was all he knew how to do. He knew, with God's help, it would work this time.

And eleven hundred thousand British and Empire soldiers died before he discovered it wasn't working.

The same delusional mentality afflicts those who espouse 'fair trade' and abominate protection.

They take off some tariffs and jobs are lost. They take off some more, and more jobs are lost, and factories closed. They do it some more, and the same dread things happen. And people don't move to 'some other sector of the economy'. They sit there, by their ruined factories and suddenly worthless houses, waiting for something to happen.

And ways are worked out to alter the means by which we measure unemployment. People working one hour a week are now called 'employed'. They hide the figures of the jobless. They wait for everyone to move into IT.

Then the IT bubble bursts, and there are no factories to go back to. Best become a waiter. Then the meltdown occurs, and tourists don't come any more. Global warming has made air travel bumpy, and scary, another outcome of global selling. People want to stay home.

And like General Haig the government thinks one more big push is all that's needed.

And all the tariff barriers come off.

And unemployment increases.

'We didn't go in hard enough, early enough,' the government says. 'We should have done more, sooner.'

They don't understand it was wrong to go so far, about halfway was probably right – like it was in, say, 1987 in Australia – and any further was too far.

175

And they don't understand that protection *worked* for five thousand years. Because it did as it said it would, protect jobs, protect local crops and orchards and industries. And the free-market experiment, which failed before World War I (just one more big push) and failed in the twenties (a chicken in every pot, the business of America is business, dance, little lady, dance) and failed in the eighties (greed is good, it will all trickle down) and failed in the nineties (some subprime mortgages on overvalued properties guaranteed by overseas loans will *surely* get the economy moving again), was a pretty shallow idea in the first place.

And if protection does what it says, protect jobs, and it usually does, it works.

And it's coming back anyway, so we'd better get used to it.

It was always coming back.

That, or as I argued in my previous book, 'By 2025 all one hundred and eighty-one countries will be competing equally on a level playing field for the same global markets and all *winning*.'

The biggest and shallowest Capitalism Delusion of all.

'VALID UNTIL JULY 10'

176

What is wrong with the following slogan?

'Hindenburg – the only way to fly.'

The product is good enough. Uplifted by helium, the original airship is safe, luxurious, exciting and glamorous. You fly at four hundred feet over dizzying landscapes, beautiful towns, majestic ocean cliffs. It's so steady you can stand a pencil on your armrest for ten, twelve hours without it falling over.

You can rent a stateroom and sleep in silk sheets. You can dance with your bride on the glass floor looking down at the lights of London, Paris, Berlin.

You have a top chef in the restaurant, an endless flow of champagne . . .

. . . and yet there is this difficulty. An image you've seen a dozen times of an airship burning up very quickly and the hysterical Herbert Morrison saying 'Oh the human-ity, the humanity' and screaming relatives on the tarmac watching their loved ones burn, just twenty feet up in the air.

177

So the airship is a good idea probably, but not the brand name.

'Hindenburg' is a no-no.

However you dress it up, the customers won't go there.

It's like saying 'Auschwitz – the entertainment capital of Poland'.

The customers won't go there.

This is pretty much what's happening to 'Global Free Trade' lately. And 'neo-liberalism'. And 'the level playing field'. And 'the deregulated free market'. And the idea that 'big government is the problem, not the solution'. And 'greed is good'.

The penny has dropped and the people are mad as hell and they're not going to take any more what the CEOs (on ten thousand dollars a day) are getting away with.

And the whole thing, like the Hindenburg, is going up in flames.

Was there a moment when it could have been saved?

I don't think so.

It was wrong at its heart from the start.

178

While writing this chapter the author encountered in a bar in Sydney the captain of the Zimbabwe Test cricket team, a black man called Prosper Utseya, who showed me a billion-dollar note. I asked what this notable product of

Mugabe's inflation was worth. 'Five dollars,' he said in a very deep voice, 'but not for long.'

On the banknote, which looked like many another banknote, was the inscription 'Valid until July 10'.

179

This phenomenon of deciduous money, incredibly shrinking money, in an era of incredibly shrinking Michigan house prices, incredibly shrinking Lehman Brothers shares, which went in a day from fourteen dollars fifteen cents to seven dollars seventy-nine cents, led me to wonder what currency one should invest, say, a million dollars, if one had it, in today.

Gold, which when I was a boy was fourteen pounds an ounce, that is, twenty-eight dollars an ounce, was now nine hundred and eighty dollars an ounce.

Water, which was pretty much free then, was if spring-derived now two dollars twenty-five cents a litre, twice the price of petrol at the pump.

Diamonds had held their value through decades of artificial scarcity, and were now four thousand one hundred and thirty dollars for a flawless one-carat white stone.

And heroin, abundantly available because of America's refusal to bomb the poppy fields of Afghanistan (which grew ninety-two percent of the world's supply) was now, on the streets of New York, worth a hundred and seventy dollars a spoonful.

If, however, the poppy fields were bombed and the farmers encouraged at gunpoint to grow apples, the price of crystal meth, cocaine and Ecstasy, which were easier to manufacture in secrecy, would go up and perhaps double in value, obeying the immutable laws of supply and demand that economic fundamentalists live by.

180

If one looks at heroin as *currency*, though, and there is no reason why one shouldn't, certain elements of practical capitalism become more plain.

One is the mark-up as the product moves from country to country.

The peasant sells a kilo of poppy resin in Kabul for four hundred and eighty dollars. This is eventually sold to a dealer in New York for eighty-seven *thousand* dollars or so. If 'cut' with powdered milk, which is cheaply purchased, the price per kilo rises to around a quarter of a million.

This seventy-four thousand one hundred and twenty-five percent mark-up is illustrative of 'market forces at work', and the immense attraction of deregulation, which allows you first-class heroin at twelve dollars twenty-five cents a hit, or one hundred and seventy-one dollars sixty per gram. This contrasts with England, where, in a government-funded 'shooting gallery', you can get the same high-quality hit, this time medically safe, for nothing, though this price range passes on, alas, less profit to the supplier.

Which is another way of saying that heroin, deregulated and 'cut' with powdered milk, varies dangerously and can kill you.

Which is, in turn, a way of saying, once more, the 'free market' can kill you.

181

And the cost, in grief and family trauma, and funeral arrangements, and the transport of the corpse home to Milwaukee and so on, can be greater than at first seems the case when shooting up joyfully in a dance-hall toilet at sixteen.

There is a social cost as well.

And the loss of a lifetime of the corpse's taxes, and the goods and services he might otherwise purchase later on.

The poetry he might write, the computer chip he might invent, and so on.

What you might, if you were not an economist, call incalculable waste.

THE VARYING PRICE OF A
BERLIN PROSTITUTE

182

In the 1970s, paper currencies varied.

An Indonesian rupiah, for instance, was worth only 0.24 American cents.

This meant an American tourist in Bali could live in a losmen, or boarding house, for five dollars a week and his landlord could feed both his guest and his family of seven for the same five dollars.

The landlord could not house and feed his family in New York, however, for ten dollars, but ten dollars in Bali went a long way.

As currencies merged, however, and the dollar became more universal, and the yen, and the euro, people began to starve.

A Rwandan hotelier needing to pay his cooks and barmen and cleaning women substantial wages in American dollars would find, after the massacres, few tourists coming to Rwanda any more and go out of business. Had he been able to pay them in Rwandan francs, which were then worth about one hundred to the US dollar, he could have stayed in business. And they could have continued to feed their families and not starve to death.

The old currency exchange rate was inequitable. But it was also merciful.

183

Is a Common Currency a good thing? Should the English pound be abandoned and replaced by the euro?

Or are there dangers in this free market of money, as there are in Africa, where no-one has the dollars that will pay for the AIDS drugs that will save their children's lives?

And people die of the currency difference? And the dollar's power in the world?

184

A famous song of the 1940s made mention of the currency problems of that era in the following lyric:

If you ever go down Trinidad
They make you feel so very glad,
Calypso sing and make up rhyme,
Guarantee you one real good fine time.

Drinkin' rum and Coca-Cola
Go down Point Koomahnah,
Both mother and daughter
Workin' for the Yankee dollar.

It was banned from the American airwaves, of course, being too evocative of the exchange rate, and the misery, and the moral compromises, it engendered.

185

When the Berlin Wall came down, and two different economies became the same economy, and two currencies merged, it was found by those interested that the East Berlin prostitutes charged for their similar services one-third the price of West Berlin prostitutes, whose prices, in competition, came down too.

This meant the household budgets of the free-market hookers were gravely impaired. And so were the household budgets of the former communist hookers, whose apartment rents, encouraged by the capitalist example a mere mile away, went up along lines of supply and demand.

186

In the 'inequitable' exchange rates of Bali in the 1970s and East Berlin in the Cold War era and Rwanda after the massacres we see, going this way and that, the same arguments on tariffs discussed earlier.

A currency crossing a border is taxed, and its price marked up, in order to make the local currency more attractive, because it supplies goods at a lower price both to tourists and natives.

When the local currency is abolished or weakened or, as in the case of Zimbabwe, made ludicrous, people starve. When people starve political instability occurs, police crackdowns, army coups. Or, in the case of Germany, Nazism.

187

When the German mark tumbled in value in the 1920s, and tumbled so far that people were seen with wheelbarrow-loads of banknotes going off to the grocer to buy their week's provisions and entire life savings were spent in this way in a month or two of frantic buying, Adolf Hitler's National Socialist party contested the 1932 elections and, using the people's money-anger, won office by fair democratic means in a coalition government that, after difficult negotiations, was eventually headed by Hitler in March 1933.

The Third Reich followed, the persecution of the Jews, an attempt to conquer mainland Europe and parts of Africa, and fifty million people died.

So in this case it seems, in the early 1930s, the free movement across borders of deregulated capital, a lack of significant tariffs and a consequent free market in variable currency did not result in a level playing field.

It resulted in a killing field.

Prove that I lie.

LUCK BE A LADY TONIGHT

188

Fundamental to the thinking of the free-trading globalist neo-liberals (Hayek, Friedman, Greenspan) is that people will act, or almost always act, if they have the information, in tactical, reasoned, logical defence of their own best economic interests.

But any gambling casino shows this is not so. Millionaire high-rollers flying into Vegas, Hong Kong, London, Tasmania, squander fortunes achieved by their family businesses, roll dice or play blackjack round the clock or watch the ball on a roulette wheel *daring the deity, praying to him, to do them a favour this time.*

Luck be a lady tonight. (Australia's richest mogul Kerry Packer once lost eight million pounds in one wild weekend among the gaming clubs of London, and was obliged, it is said, to steal his *own gold bullion from his own office safe* and demand its value back from the insurance company to recoup his titanic losses and his famous losing streak.)

What these jet-setting dipsticks do, and many of them are CEOs, is not logical, defensive, tactical or reasoned, but superstitious, religious, unhinged. Delusional. It does not defend their own self-interest, or that of their heirs and successors, but *gambles the family silver* on the roll of a dice, the fall of a card.

They know the odds are stacked against them, they have seen *Casablanca*, everyone has seen *Casablanca*, and yet they go there. And they bet their money on a rolling ball on a spinning wheel for eight or ten hours of champagne-drinking and endless frenzy in buildings in which the downstairs freezers are stacked with the corpses of recent suicides.

And how can men who do this, and also run companies, be said to have different instincts when negotiating global mergers, doing business with Communist China or estimating the value of worldwide assets on which they borrow money? Were Ken Lay and Jeff Skilling, and Alan Bond and James Goldsmith, and Conrad Black and Rodney Adler sober defenders of their corporations' profit margin, or so many toey Sky Mastersons crooning luck be a lady tonight and going for broke?

That most people *don't* act in their own self-interest, *and if they don't the economic fundamentalist thesis falls over*, is shown on any racecourse thronged with gamblers, or any football club agog with poker machines, or any glass tabernacle full of true believers in a heaven they have never seen.

189

Wealthy true believers, some of them, shovelling loads of money at a predatory coke-sniffing charlatan like Ted Haggard, or a pompous, adulterous tub of lard like Jimmy Swaggart or, in slightly different architecture, the Pope. Instead of having their accountants and auditors check out this Heaven that is promised, they take it as read, yelling hallelujahs and murmuring thoughtful prayers, crossing themselves in front of a statue of a virgin *with five children*, believing in a Hell full of eternally frying Muslims, trusting in an institution full of pederasts and robe-wearing, bell-jangling sodomites adamant that no-one dare have sexual intercourse who doesn't want babies and drinking human blood and eating human flesh is a good investment in an eternity of singing hymns and saying *holy, holy, holy, Lord God Almighty* to a testy old deity who once proposed to drown the lot of us for bad behaviour.

And global economics' primary thesis is that *four billion adult people as credulous as this*, including twenty million apprentice suicide bombers, will act in their own *self-interest* as defined in columns of profit and loss by Moody's and Standard & Poor's.

If this is not true then nothing connected with deregulating economies can be true either. These four billion dice-rolling, hymn-hollering, shrine-kissing, breast-beating fools are, like Solzhenitsyn's definition of the Russians, 'a mob in search of a whip'.

Which is another way of saying, surely, 'in need of regulation'.

190

Perhaps the greatest proof that people do not act in their own self-interest lies in the persecution of the Jews.

Many Jews in the fifteenth century were given a choice of embracing Christianity or being disembowelled.

Many chose the latter. And so died, howling.

Their fates would make some sense if they truly believed that on the other side of this horrible death was a golden city with crystal gates and pearly streams and lions and lambs gladly frolicking together.

But most Jews don't believe in this kind of heaven, or life after death at all. After death you 'sleep in the bosom of Abraham', insensibly dwell in the house of your fathers, the shared memory of your tribe, and that is that.

Why then did they not convert, or pretend to convert, and prolong the life they had? Their one life on earth?

Why did they not act in their own self-interest?

Beats me.

And they are the ones who are supposed to be good at practical economics. They are the ones who invented (with a few WASP collaborators) neo-liberalism, and neo-conservatism.

Why did they do that?

191

Another difficulty with this theory of a level playing field over which naked self-interest equally flows is that eight hundred million of the humans who take part in it don't believe in lending or borrowing money at interest.

These are those Muslims who think it the work of Satan. This is why some of them hit with hijacked planes the *World Trade Center*, a den of capitalist devils.

'And what you give in interest that it may increase on people's wealth, increases not with Allah's permission,' says the Koran.

This would seem to me to constitute a worry. Global economics has to cover the globe, or it can't really work. And if eight hundred million of its potential customers are determined to blow it up, consign it to an everlasting lake of fire, its implementation may face inconvenient delays.

One of these is piracy.

192

Piracy, like terrorism, has much in common with global economics – the targeted raids, the swift withdrawals, the asset-stripping, the murderous threats, the holding of people to ransom.

Once called 'privateering' it was *licensed* by Elizabeth I to harass Spanish shipping, burn Cádiz, carry off their ill-gotten gold of which the Monarch demanded a vast percentage – behaving, in fact, like Macquarie Bank in the early twenty-first century.

But a more primal piracy is now afflicting the Gulf of Suez and, consequently, world trade.

As I write this chapter Barack Obama is wisely not declaring a 'War on Piracy' as his predecessor might have done but sending in a number of battleships to discourage this outbreak of post-colonial Muslim free enterprise which, true to Allah's purpose, does not lend money, but only takes it.

193

It is not hard to see why piracy is currently so disliked: it disrupts international commerce and, by boarding civilian vessels and kidnapping people, pirates endanger life.

But piracy has killed in the past year very few people indeed, fewer people by far than global fundamentalism – five million one hundred and ninety-nine thousand, nine hundred and eighty-nine people fewer than smoking has killed for instance, three hundred and sixty-seven thousand, nine hundred and eighty-nine fewer than heroin and, if Gordon Brown is to be believed, three hundred and ninety-nine thousand nine hundred and eighty-nine fewer children than Lehman Brothers' collapse and the world meltdown it triggered will cost humanity in the next year or two.

And *Somalian* piracy, it might be argued, only seizes

back some of the ill-gotten wealth in tens of trillions of dollars which English, German, French and Belgian colonial officials and American slave traders and AIDS drug purveyors and Dutch diamond miners illegally gouged from the African continent in the last three centuries.

It is a small-scale American War of Independence, you might say, by an equivalent of the New England farmers, merchants and sailors who turned Boston Harbor into a teapot. It is an assertion of the anger of the exploited underclass of the sort that Che, Simón Bolivar, Toussaint Louverture and Robin of Locksley, also known as Robin Hood, once roused to testy, violent revolt.

194

Or that is what its public relations people, its Alastair Campbells and Tony Snows might say.

It is actually, in fact, economic fundamentalism by other means, by more vivid and headline-grabbing means. Like global economics it targets the situationally vulnerable and deprives them of their wealth and property. Like economic fundamentalism it holds to ransom small merchants of exportable goods and their ill-paid underlings, and sometimes causes their deaths.

It has done this so well that a good number of ships may not go through the Suez Canal any more, and whole Middle Eastern economies in the tourist towns of Aden, Alexandria, Port Said, Beirut and Haifa in the business of shipping goods from Rome to India, from Tokyo to Europe, will be impoverished. The effect will be like that of the Asian tsunami, the Chinese earthquake, the fires of Delphi and London tourism after the bombing of the underground in 2005, a devastation of trade, a massive act of economic cheating, of market sabotage on a global scale.

The sort of thing the international free market does all the time.

Your money or your life.

195

It turns out military snipers took out three of the pirates while rescuing Captain Phillips, I have just heard on the news.

The executives of Lehman Brothers and AIG, however, are still at large.

196

The Lehman Brothers executives were last seen carrying cardboard boxes full of memorabilia out of a skyscraper in New York, mourning a fine old company that had been in business since 1850.

Army snipers did not shoot them though they did more harm (it would seem) than the pirates, causing indirectly (it could be argued) more than fifty thousand deaths.

This is because under US law *corporations* are what do

harm, and, since they are abstract entities, they cannot be imprisoned for what they do, though they can be fined. And no-one in the corporation can be imprisoned either, not even the CEO, for crimes against humanity, though they can be arrested, and dealt with severely, as Ken Lay was, and Jeff Skilling, for cooking the books.

Alan Bond served three whole years for stealing a billion dollars.

Discuss.

197

This disproportion of crime and punishment (a young black man gets twenty-five years for stealing, over time, despite warnings, three pizzas, and an old white man gets a three–hundred-million-dollar bonus for disrupting, bruising and sometimes ruining a hundred thousand lives) is a visible reminder, of course, of the days of slavery and colonial oppression.

In Australia in 2000 a black teenager was gaoled for stealing some coloured pencils, textas and tubes of paint with which he hoped to draw some greeting cards to send to his distant Aboriginal family, and became so depressed by his incarceration he hanged himself from a knotted grey blanket in his cell.

And it is a reminder, too, of the system known in England, and known for centuries, as Class.

198

In England in 1800 a nine-year-old child would be sent by his impoverished parents to pick pockets in a crowded Soho street. If apprehended, he would be quickly brought to court and there sentenced to hang. The execution would be public, and his parents would attend. The jury convicting him would often weep as they did so.

But they were convinced they had no choice: the wealth of the rich must be protected at all costs, even if it involved the taking of the life of a child. If it was not protected, the Lower Orders would be encouraged to seek it in this way instead of doing useful work as domestic servants, bargees, vendors of periwinkles or fiddle-playing buskers in the Strand.

The Higher Orders, by contrast, did no work at all. They lived off the earnings of their vast estates, on their slave-tended sugar and tobacco plantations in the West Indies, spending their ample excess wealth on theatre-going, private orchestras, grand balls, card-playing and Grand Tours of Europe that took sometimes two years. The men wore perfume, powdered wigs and 'beauty spots' over their pimples or facial disfigurements. They wore velvet jackets, laced shirts, stockings and sometimes corsets, and kept at the ready leather contraceptives they used over and over. If moved to do so, they would 'tumble' a housemaid, and if she became pregnant, sack her from the household, refuse her a reference and force her into prostitution in the streets.

It is the contention of this book that this attitude has not wholly abated in the rich. The Lower Orders are expendable still.

And once gone, it will seem they had never existed.

199

It is thought, looking back at the question of Class, that ignorance of contraception was part of the trouble.

The Lower Orders had as many as fifteen children and, in crowded basement flats with two other families, communicable disease would kill in infancy five or six of them.

In times of fiscal downturn or market failure the breadwinner might lose his job in the blacking factory and with it his sixpence a day and be forced to prostitute his twelve-year-old daughter or send, as we have seen, his nine-year-old son to pick pockets in a crowd, and later regret this beneath the gallows on Tyburn Hill.

Many charitable thinkers in those days abominated the society that caused these things, and hanged so many children. But they believed it was the way things were. People could be asked to be more kindly but there was nothing, legislatively, they could do.

There was no alternative.

TINA.

Or, as Rupert Murdoch used to say, GOTCHA.

ARISE YE WORKERS FROM YOUR SLUMBERS

200

It was wages of threepence a day for a sixteen-hour day and a six-day week, and children working for tuppence a day in foul-smelling factories till they dropped dead at the loom at the age of ten, that caused the rise of the Union Movement.

Strikes were organised, unionists gaoled, some of them, the Tolpuddle Martyrs, sent to Australia for smashing machinery that took away the Lower Orders' jobs, Sunday-school teachers moved to form in the Welsh and English and Scottish chapels various labour guilds. After the 1867 Reform Act, which enfranchised all male householders, parliamentary representation was sought by unionists educated in Schools of Arts and Railway Institutes, and an affiliation, the Fabian Society, of upper-middle-class intellectuals that over time through parliamentary harassment brought on a forty-hour week, an average wage of one pound eight shillings, and free primary education in 1891, an old-age pension, in 1908, of five shillings a week and, after a lot of parliamentary commotion, universal health care in Great Britain in 1946.

This was enacted by the Union Movement's political wing, the Labour Party. Noting its considerable successes, and its itchy determination to get the Lower Orders safe workplaces, fair wages, good housing, clean cities, good local schools and overtime pay, the Conservative Party under Margaret Thatcher determined to destroy the Union Movement.

The way you do.

201

It was suggested by the Thatcherites that the Union Movement had served its purpose and should now disband.

Workers' conditions and salaries were now as good as they were ever going to get, and all agitation for a better life on earth should now cease and desist among the Lower Orders. Their unreasonable demands that the mines stay open and their communities remain intact as long as the coal was making money (which it was) were daily, and yearly and unforgivably, she said, eroding the British economy, and the right to strike, which was a kind of economic treason, should be severely diminished if not done away with altogether.

202

In the fine film *Brassed Off* we see what a closing mine does to men's pride, their communities, their marriages and even their music. We wonder why, when they were *still* making money, Thatcher closed eighty-four coal mines. The coal could have been piled up and sold to China for billions, trillions even, in this last decade. The men could have kept their houses and marriages and sense of self. But she cast them out, into street begging, busking, ill-paying drab jobs packing supermarket shelves. Or, as another good film *The Full Monty* shows, male striptease on hens' nights.

The coal towns dwindled, the brass bands, choirs, pub culture, football teams passed into grumpy disintegrating legend. A way of life was lost – as we see, too, in *Billy Elliot* – and nothing was gained except a few more noughts on some Superpersons' bottom lines. And a reputation in Margaret Thatcher for being 'ballsy'.

The Union Movement, smashed, grew bitter and fratricidal, their leaders, like Arthur Scargill, corrupt and fond of caviar-and-Rolls-Royce living and beautifully sculpted hairpieces. When Tony Blair got in, he made damn sure no morning teas occurred at Number 10 with union bosses any more, as they had under Harold Wilson. He knew 'the unions' usefulness had passed'.

He knew there was no alternative.

And he admired Margaret Thatcher with the keenness of a choirboy singing for the Pope.

And two hundred thousand good lives were lost, their towns denuded of creative energy, good music, good hometown feeling.

And what was gained?

A big, significant victory for economic fundamentalism, that's all.

And canonical status among conservative economists for Margaret Thatcher.

203

This was a horrible woman. The author followed her around in 1983.

She had a widow's hump, a bald patch, a wig, capped teeth, empurpled gums, a painful, fraudulent, whispery voice artificially deepened by minders who hated her initial shriek, great legs, enormous charisma, a working substitute for female beauty, a fondness for midnight whisky and, in part because of it, *a passionate conviction she knew all that she needed to know.*

She rarely went to the theatre, saw films, read fiction, listened with interest to music or watched the BBC, but she knew what she needed to know. She knew there was no alternative.

And she privatised the electricity.

'You can't do that,' said her amiable, thoughtful Deputy Leader, Willie Whitelaw. 'Electricity is, well, fundamental. It's a national resource.'

'You watch me,' she said.

And she did it, and got away with it – in part because the Labour Party split, and its vote went two ways and she was able to win with forty-two percent, in part because she mismanaged her way into a war in the Falklands where lots of brave Tommies died, in part because the Labour leader, Michael Foot, a brilliant, charming man and a wonderful writer, came across as a doddering old fool because of a road-accident injury which made him lurch when he walked.

204

And the electricity was privatised, and a hole plugged in the Budget, and some debt written off, and all over Europe it was realised *she had gotten away with it.*

And the leaders of Europe started privatising things too, a train service here, a health fund there, a bus line, a wharf-loading facility, a steelworks, a telco, a prison . . .

And the age, the golden age of the CEO began.

There was no alternative.

205

The logic of all this was that government didn't need to own those things any more, since private enterprise would run them 'more efficiently', meaning they'd sack a lot of people, and the price of things would *come down,* it was said. And all government had to do was watch them carefully, make sure they were honourably and safely run.

Aha, said the economic fundamentalists, here's a go.

206

And they told the governments, Not so fast. We'll buy these entities from you, but not until they're state-of-the-art and making *a lot of money*. So you *improve* them, and we'll *consider* buying them.

And the dumbfounded governments did this, then found themselves in a room full of lawyers.

Our clients will only buy these entities if they come with a lot of freedoms, said the lawyers, not with government busybodies nosing into things.

But – but – but, the governments protested, *that* was the original idea, *that* was what we promised the people, that privatised trains would be *safe*, that airlines wouldn't *crash*, that bus lines wouldn't close down the remote and little-used services.

The more fool you, said the lawyers. All *that's* got to go for a start.

And they put in thousands of clauses, penalty clauses that guaranteed that if they stuffed up or killed people or injured people and the government tried to de-license them, *the government would have to give them a whole lot of money.*

In New South Wales, for instance, a deal was made between the state government and Cross-City Motorway Pty Ltd to build a transit tunnel under the city for motorcars. One of the provisos was that the government block off a lot of suburban streets to make sure commuters used it, although it was very short. Another one was that it was not the government but Cross-City Motorway that borrowed the eight hundred million dollars it took to build it, though the government could have borrowed the money at a lower rate of interest and therefore charged less toll to pay it back.

Another one was that if the whole thing failed the government would give their private partners eight hundred million dollars.

Well, the toll was four dollars, or one dollar seventy per kilometre, one of the most expensive tolls in the world, and the tunnel very short, and the suburban people were incensed to be paying four dollars for a journey (admittedly a briefer one) that they used to make for free. So they boycotted the tunnel and drove the long way round, and the whole thing failed in a couple of months. And Cross-City Motorway got eight hundred million dollars back from their government partners, a lot of which paid executive fees in substantial amounts for their incompetence, as the Invisible Hand intended.

One of these executives was Nick Greiner, the former Premier of New South Wales, the one who'd instituted perpetual misery on the overnight sleeping trains where nobody slept much, including the author.

His successor, John Fahey, sold the Bank of New South Wales for less than it earned in a year, once you shook down the subclauses and the annual penalty payback provisions of the sale contract, a net sum of two hundred million dollars. When the Commonwealth Bank took it over, it was valued at two billion dollars. Which meant the government could have got ten times the amount it was sold for, and chose not to. Funny, that.

These privatised entities were usually shonky. The various companies that took over lots of British Rail had forty-six train accidents and 'incidents' (fires, derailments, crashes) in fifteen years and ninety-seven passenger deaths. The privatised Thames Water ensured the deaths by typhus of several old women whose water they cut off *within three days of them not paying the final notices*. ABC Learning, a corporate chain of child-care preschools in Australia (whose CEO Eddy Groves paid himself six hundred and ninety-seven thousand dollars in the year before it crashed), though subsidised by the government to the tune of seven thousand five hundred per year per child, posted a loss of four hundred and thirty-seven million dollars in 2008 and had to be bailed out by the government while Eddy Groves (or so it is alleged) amassed and protected loads of his property, chuckling to himself.

And a lot of working parents have nowhere to put their kids now, and these kids are being emotionally deprived and intellectually stunted, because of the company bottom line. Gotcha, as Rupert and Margaret would say.

Gotcha.

207

And the Golden Age of privatised monopoly wealth and self-indulgence went on for quite a while. Five years before declaring bankruptcy, Alan Bond was on *BRW* magazine's Rich List as having four hundred million dollars. James Goldsmith amassed 2.5 billion dollars in personal wealth. Ken Lay, CEO of Enron, got two hundred and fifty million a year. Sol Trujillo of Telstra got thirty-one million in wages, and two hundred and fifty thousand shares, *and six hundred and twenty-one thousand two hundred and seventy-five dollars in relocation fees.*

Relocation fees. It was enough, in those days, for a modest, penny-watching couple to retire on.

And that was just Sol moving house.

208

Some of the deals they bullied and blasted out of ashen and shamefaced and cowardly governments were truly spectacular.

Doug Moran, who'd made his pile from aged-care facilities, had legislation passed so he could charge old people who booked into his retirement villages *whatever he liked.*

It wasn't put exactly like that, more like the Marxist formulation *from each according to his capacity, to each according to his need.*

The legislation said Doug could seize from you *whatever your house was worth*, it might be a hundred and twenty thousand dollars, it might be sixty thousand, it might be six hundred thousand (a lot of money in those days), as a fair price for dying – soon, please – in one of his neat little flats in one of his bright little twilight mausoleums for the quietly fading, gullible old of Australia.

Australia didn't like this much. If their dads and mums were in for this it was bad enough, but they also knew, or suspected they knew, or eventually came to conclude that they knew, *that they themselves* would be old pretty soon, and Doug would seize and pillage their family home as he did their mum's.

And Doug's friend John Howard, the Prime Minister, was forced to overturn his own bill, and nearly lost office when fifty-one percent of the nation voted against him in 1998.

209

You will note from the examples thus far in the book that capitalism hangs around, loitering with intent, the things we most need and makes a lot of money from them: things like a roof, and warmth, and water, and parking space, and treatment for sickness, and old-age care. Things we can't do without.

And if you used this formula a bit you might say economic fundamentalism, and maybe capitalism altogether, exploits our addictions – to cigarettes, to beer, to the sight of a female thigh, to a view of water and avoidance of falling rain, a remembered surge of pleasure at land viewed from water, from the deck of a boat, or melodies you can dance to.

Capitalism thrives on addiction, which is why it makes much of its money from selling drugs and young girls' penetrable bodies and like any exploiter of addictions it should be controlled, regulated.

Punished, even.

Or am I wrong?

210

On Saturday, January 20th, 2001, after a good deal of uncomfortable vote-rigging and a Supreme Court decision, the Capitalism Delusion's best news arrived in the White House.

His name was George W. Bush.

He came from the Texas oil business, as did his Vice President, Dick Cheney, his eventual Secretary of Defense, Robert Gates, and his National Security Adviser, Condoleezza Rice.

He had failed in the oil business himself, but he felt he had a good nose for capitalist practice, and what it needed was less punishment and less regulation.

He brought the top tax rate for corporations down, in varying amounts depending on their size and usefulness, and the top tax rate for seriously rich Americans down from 24.2 percent to 19.6 percent. He declared Arctic wildernesses should be open for oil drilling. He cancelled legislation limiting how much corporations could pollute. He brought real wages, already piteously low, down by one percent, leaving millions of working stiffs on five dollars fifteen cents an hour.

And he provided America's biggest corporations with the thing they wanted most.

A war.

211

After one Egyptian, one Lebanese, two Emirates and fifteen Saudi Arabians attacked and brought down New York's Twin Towers and punched a hole in the Pentagon, he sent in formidable ships and rockets and fighter planes to attack, not Egypt, the Emirates, Lebanon or Saudi Arabia, but a much less well-armed country, Afghanistan, on the sure and certain knowledge that Osama bin Laden, who may or may not have had something to do with the attack, was living there, or perhaps in Pakistan.

Mud villages were pulverised, schoolhouses levelled, hospitals destroyed and a hundred thousand people, maybe, killed and many wounded who, for the want of efficient ambulances, died too.

'We'll smoke him out,' he said. 'We'll get him running.'

In order to make his task a little harder, he let twenty-four of Osama bin Laden's blood relatives leave America *two days after the attack, on 9/13, while all other planes were grounded*, on two special flights lest they help the army find out where their brother, nephew or cousin might be.

The army pretty soon found out anyway. He was in a particular cave in the Tora Bora mountain region. The British had him surrounded and Bush ordered them to let him go.

Why did he do this?

212

The probable explanation was that if bin Laden was captured or killed, there'd be no strong reason to stay round Afghanistan bombing mud huts and using up valuable weaponry any more, the weaponry that big corporations were making a packet out of, or kicking down and rebuilding towns and delivering hamburgers which Cheney's company, Halliburton, was good at. Cheney had been Halliburton's CEO only six months before and he had four hundred and thirty-three thousand shares in it.

Nor would he have been able, or easily able, to install Hamid Karzai, an oil man himself and part of the Union Oil Company of California, as President and get *an oil pipeline put through Afghanistan to the Caspian Sea*, an outcome he had his heart set on.

So the war was prolonged and is going on till this day. It has cost so far eight hundred and fifty-two billion dollars in money borrowed from the Chinese because Bush spent Bill Clinton's one–hundred-and-twenty-seven-billion-dollar surplus pretty fast, and now the US is losing it – losing the war, I mean – it may go on for another ten years before they find some face-saving way of giving it back to the Taliban and going home.

This shoddy exercise, though, is a bonanza for the economic fundamentalists, who, as they liked to, sucked the government dry, charging hundreds of billions of dollars for services unnecessary in peacetime.

213

Bush then went to war in Iraq, claiming its leader was going to bomb with nuclear weapons an unknown fraction of the world pretty soon, declaring this war would be over fast, *and it would pay for itself when they got their hands on the oil.*

They were so keen on the oil they guarded the Oil Ministry's building while the Museum was looted of Biblical treasures and the great National Library and Archives, and its irreplaceable gold-embossed seventh-century texts, burnt down.

But the price soon outran all the oil they could pump out of the desert in defiance of the sabotage of the 'Saddam diehards' who blew up the derricks and breached the oil pipelines and set them on fire, and six years later, longer than World War II, it's still going on, the diehards haven't died yet, and it's cost each US taxpayer six thousand four hundred and twelve dollars thus far, plus interest, I guess, on the Chinese loans.

It should be emphasised that all this money is going, in the main, to American corporations whom the American government, Obama's too, is daily rewarding in scores of millions *for their lack of success*.

214

It is hard *not* to believe that there are certain powerful figures who want these two wars to run as long as they can.

None of this World War II nonsense, old friend, when between the attack on Pearl Harbor and the Japanese surrender there was only forty-five months.

This is *real* money we're making.

We need longer wars.

215

No more striking example of this exists than what Naomi Klein described in her fine book *The Shock Doctrine* as 'disaster capitalism', in her discussion on Hurricane Katrina and Milton Friedman.

Friedman, then aged ninety-four, proposed in what proved to be his final article that New Orleans' many damaged public schools be *not* rebuilt but replaced with vouchers for pupils who would go instead to newly established 'charter schools', privately run and profit-making.

What a good idea, the city fathers thought, and while most of the city's poorer residents were still in exile in caravan parks up north in Baton Rouge and Biloxi, legislation was forced through and public rescue money seized, buildings demolished and land sold off, and within nineteen months the one hundred and twenty-three public schools were reduced in number to three, and the seven charter schools enlarged in number to thirty-one, and the forty-nine hundred public schoolteachers, members of a once-strong union, effectively sacked from their jobs. Public education was thereby abolished pretty much overnight in New Orleans in 2006 by a hit squad of rapid-response investment capitalists, colluding (as always) with corrupted government officials in a form of daylight robbery.

And the razed school sites, along with much of the public housing, were 'redeveloped' as condominiums and shopping malls and up-market tourist facilities with water views.

The way the Invisible Hand intended.

216

Friedman died soon after this, his last great victory as Grand Marshal of Greed in its unending war with democracy. It showed what he long had said, that 'only a crisis – actual or perceived – produces real change. When that crisis occurs, the actions that are taken depend on the ideas that are lying around. That, I believe, is our basic function: to develop alternatives to existing policies, to keep them alive and available until the politically impossible becomes politically inevitable.'

To move quickly, in short, before the crisis-smashed society slipped back into the 'tyranny of the status quo'.

He said this too when advising General Pinochet in Chile after his coup and Allende's suicide. 'Economic shock treatment,' he called it. And right-wing programmes, rapidly enacted, followed catastrophe after catastrophe thereafter along the lines of his leaping-jackal theory.

They did so after 9/11 in New York, and after Shock and Awe in Baghdad. In each case a great city centre was pulverised, a society up-ended, its values rewritten, its weapons manufacturers and 'security firms' enriched and its human rights (for the moment) suspended or assaulted, jeered at or belittled, Guantanamo and Abu Ghraib filled with random swarms of prisoners indiscriminately tortured, stripped naked and menaced with dogs, because 'the situation has changed' and 'the world will never be the same again' after this convenient catastrophe, this consequent and necessary New World Order.

217

Likewise after the Asian tsunami, the devastated seaside villages of Sri Lanka were not rebuilt but seized overnight by government edict and 'redeveloped' as tourist resort hotels, their now homeless and boatless fisher-folk dispersed aghast into exile and their communities, after a thousand years of genial cohabitation and proud tradition, ended overnight, abolished, gazumped, unwelcome here, keep out.

Disaster Capitalism, like the jackal, lies in wait for a convenient death, and then it strikes with ferocity, precision and carnivorous force – and collusive government assistance, of course – and speedily passes new laws that allow it into the wreckage, sniffing and yelping with eager hope among the drowned corpses and floating blackboards, the splintered classrooms of someone's Old School, fresh fodder now for the predatory, roving, well-heeled and well-connected adventurer. Someone's old school will do. Someone's old house will do. Anything will do.

Socialism for the deserving rich, as Gore said, and free enterprise for the undeserving poor.

<h2 style="text-align:center">218</h2>

It is hard though, too, to describe what has happened in the last few pages as 'unfettered global economics' or 'free market capitalism' or 'global free trade' because government, and Big Government, is so much intertwined with it.

It has to be what Gore Vidal called it, 'Socialism for the deserving rich, and free enterprise for the undeserving poor.'

THE HUMAN FACTOR

219

Yet despite all the help it got from timorous compliant governments that shuffled hundreds of billions of poker chips its way, it came unstuck, it melted down, it proved a delusion after all, in America at least. America is like a man down to his jockstrap in a game of strip-poker holding a pair of threes and trying to keep a straight face.

How, apart from stupidity, did all this happen to a 'can-do' culture, a 'know-how' country, a nation built on migrant ingenuity, vast natural resources and no mainland war damage for the entire twentieth century?

220

Well . . . it forgot a few things about human nature.

One is that you don't buy a new car every year even though it looks different from last year's car. Since the auto industry is the lever that lifts the entire economy, the tourism, the petrol stations, the car-parks by the shopping malls, the wife's independence, the firstborn son's most exciting birthday present, the weekends away in a shack in the mountains, the helicopter shots of police pursuing O.J. Simpson's white Ford Bronco, it's important the auto assembly lines keep going and keep employing people.

But they didn't.

People kept their old cars for eight years, then bought second-hand replacement cars. They turned away from big-finned gas-guzzlers to the meeker, tinier Japanese models. The government meanwhile let in with low tariffs Volkswagens, Toyotas, Hondas that cost less to run and didn't tempt urban vandals to scratch their duco.

The auto giants made too many of them, too fast, and watched them crowd the saleyards unbought for years on end.

They suppressed the Tucker, a good car. They suppressed the old electric cars, the new electric ones, the cars that ran on water, on air, on half the petrol a Mini-Minor needs. They bought up the patents and kept silence on these wonderful new inventions.

And they let the world overtake them.

They made cars too expensive for their auto workers to purchase out of loyalty. Henry Ford never made that mistake, but Henry Ford II did.

And they imagined patriotism would sustain them against the onslaught of cheaper cars of better quality.

221

It's uncertain why they did this – if Robert McNamara had stayed at Ford after 1960, one feels, the history of cars would have been mightily different – but it's likely Big Oil had a hand in it.

Big Oil liked selling petrol to big cars with big fins that soaked up lots of it.

Big Oil arranged (as that fine social documentary *Who Framed Roger Rabbit* stirringly demonstrates) that LA's excellent transit system be dug up and junked and replaced with ever-soaring cloverleaf highways on which more and more motorists drove more and more miles from distant places to their office very quickly in gas-guzzling Chryslers and Studebakers, cloverleaf high-ways on which no healthy commuting bicyclist dared risk his life.

Big Oil (as we have seen) sought oil outside America and instructed various Presidents to ally themselves with South American dictators, Saudi monarchies, Shahs and Czars and tom-tomming cannibal chiefs to get more of it. And to overthrow social democrats like Mosaddeq to get it and restore their friend the Shah.

Big Oil made sure George W. Bush, the best friend they ever had, was twice made President though he didn't win the count either time, and Saddam Hussein was hanged, and Ahmadinejad discouraged and Hugo Chávez, with any luck, assassinated for taking their oil wells off them, 'nationalising' them (a dread word back then) and selling petrol cheap to Castro's Cuba.

One can blame Big Oil for a lot of things. Its immemorial tendencies in *There Will Be Blood*, a fine brutal film, are well portrayed.

222

But not only Big Oil but most of corporate America made the same mistake.

With an ever-swelling passion for new novelties and the ever-accelerating migrant experience of new suburbs, new bungalows, new cars, new wives, new facelifts, new self-definitions, new 'adult toys', new surnames, and new expanding shopping malls and religious experiences, they forgot how great the human need of the *familiar* is, and failed to make money out of it.

They developed the throwaway culture, the national habit of replacement not repair, of new shoes not new heels for old shoes, of new televisions not old radios you repair, and lost the essential component of any culture, which is repetition.

Human arrangements had worked this way for thousands of years, with harvest festivals, Easter pageants, midsummer-night orgies, marriage vows and family Christmas gatherings, regular exchanges of gifts between friends and debutante balls, national anthems and football songs to old tunes *repeating* age-old celebratory habits of mind.

But the New World culture of *new, new, new* began to bust that up. Not just film but sound film, then colour film, then CinemaScope, 3D, Cinerama, then television, colour television, digital television, big-screen digital television, each new stage discarding the excellent, refreshing particularities of the one before, new board games, new card games, new mechanical ways of gambling money, exploring space, teaching dolphins to suicide-bomb Russian submarines, became a kind of psychosis that had to be treated by new forms of analysis, group therapy, hug therapy, new theories of the mind. People bought guns to ease their anxieties and blam-blammed away at shooting galleries, then brought their guns home.

And much of it, not all of it, was crazy.

223

For when people did the ordinary things again – talking over wine with old friends, bushwalking and sitting by campfires, singing at family reunions, swimming in summer twilights on beaches familiar from childhood, making funny speeches at luncheon clubs, tossing a ball around between grandfather, son and grandson – they realised American *busyness*, American entrepreneurial innovative adventurousness, was largely a waste of time.

And the people didn't *buy* the big engulfing computer games, or not in sufficient numbers, and the IT bubble burst, and they went back to Scrabble, crosswords and trivia bingo and reruns on cable of old Bogart and Bette Davis movies, old Crosby and Garland musicals, old Lenny Bernstein lectures-with-orchestra, embracing repetition as a child does, wanting to hear from a parent the same story, in the same words, night after night in infancy.

Had they known of this repetition factor they may not have made so many new cars, just repaired the old ones. And they might have brought back (which they didn't) a lot of old forties movies in the fifties, year after year, in special Saturday morning sessions, or Friday midnight sessions, or outdoor screenings on late summer nights on big screens by the river, and made more money that way. And they might have filmed a lot of Babe Ruth baseball games, or Don Bradman cricket games, and reissued them year after year in sporting stadiums on the off-nights making money. But they didn't

224

For the let's-make-a-million-make-it-quick-make-it-now habit of mind precluded this. They had to get on, trash the past, do new things. They had to tear nice old sandstone tenement districts down and put up glass skyscrapers, more, more, bigger, bigger. The skyscrapers put up property prices, made deserts of the inner cities, drove the bohemians out of town, bankrupted their galleries and little theatres and small newspapers with rising rents and parking fees and water rates and property taxes and sent them into gloomy retirement at fifty-five or sixty, or death by drugs at forty.

It's what happens in a migrant culture. Every migrant story starts with a defeat; discuss.

And defeat and flight and bluster can be habit-forming; discuss.

And the entrepreneurial bluster that follows defeat and flight; discuss.

And causes economic meltdowns.

Prove that I lie.

225

One man who understood about repetition was Walt Disney. He not only re-imagined classic stories like *Snow White* and *Pinocchio* and *Cinderella* and *Mary Poppins* and *Peter Pan* and *Alice in Wonderland*, he re-imagined, in Disneyland, his home country America.

'Disneyland,' he said, 'is American history and geography with the boring bits left out.'

And, already hooked on repetition, American four-year-olds are still going to it.

226

Another thing they failed to realise was how most humans hate getting fired.

When we're fired we freeze in our tracks, we go pale, we withdraw, we lock ourselves in our room. We don't go out and buy things. Even if we get another job in a couple of weeks we may never buy things at the same rate again. Our self-esteem shrivels, and with it our audacity of hope.

Our brand-loyalty too. If we are fired by Nike and replaced by tiny Asian slaves, we may not buy that brand again, and neither will our grandchildren. If I catch you wearing a Nike shoe, we say, I'll disinherit you.

227

Another thing is the way they got accountants to run entities that required other kinds of expertise. An airline doesn't need an accountant, but a pilot or an aircraft mechanic would do fairly well (I suggest) as an airline CEO. A broadcasting and television service doesn't need a lawyer but a broadcaster, probably, or a studio director or a famous comedian who knows about audiences.

And it helps if the new boss has worked in the company before. Flying in a moron from America to, say, establish a bicameral democracy in Iraq with Sunnis and Shi-ites bringing thousand-year-old quarrels and handguns to the Cabinet room is not a good look. It looks, as Lady Bracknell might say, 'like carelessness'.

228

So is putting an accountant (or an agent) in charge of a Hollywood studio. He forms the view that Hollywood runs on stars, not noticing that *Star Wars*, *E.T.*, *Wall-E*,

Titanic, The Sound of Music, Raiders of the Lost Ark, Chariots of Fire, Lawrence of Arabia didn't have any, and the lead girl in *Gone with the Wind* was an unknown when she was cast, as was the initial lead boy in *Superman*. And they start paying stars ten, twenty million dollars to be in turkeys like *Waterworld* and *Pearl Harbor* and *The Golden Compass*, of which the budgets, *because of the star's presence*, blow out to one hundred and fifty million dollars and require two hundred million dollars of publicity and so lose money they get fired for losing, whereas a modest fifteen-million-dollar film, *Slumdog Millionaire*, about the poverty everybody is feeling wins Oscars because it's a good story and it makes half a billion overnight.

An accountant doesn't know about these things. He can't tell a good story from a bad one. He's hardly ever been to the pictures himself. He's deeply ignorant. And he's hooked on Star Theory, another version of the Invisible Hand, another example of the world-religion that is economic fundamentalism.

Another Capitalism Delusion.

229

Another one is America's religions, whose product is unproven and whose income is never taxed. So any fool self-help theory, whose product is unproven, *and therefore falsely advertised*, like Scientology for instance, can palm itself off as a religion, brainwash its infantile, self-doubting adherents, charge with kidnapping anyone who tries to rescue them, and *never be taxed*, never suffer the smallest punishment for ruining lives forever.

They are perfect examples of the unregulated free market. Why should the government bother itself with trivial matters like organised polygamous child abuse or suicidal cults like Jim Jones' Peoples Temple when customers have freely bought that product on the unregulated free market of religion?

Any other such product would attract the attention of the False Advertising laws and be closed down. But not your average American religion. Eternal life? Step right up, put your money in the plate. Eternal forgiveness for the abominable sin of incestuous rape and murder? No worries. If you just believe in Jesus and put your money in the plate. Release your ancestors from a thousand years of purgatory? Yes, siree. Just sign this document and put your money in the plate.

A great number of American business executives subscribe to this or another form of resurrection-redemption-and-forgiveness religion.

Which just goes to show how delusional they are.

230

They're delusional enough to believe, for instance, that you win Iraqis' hearts and minds by bombing and shooting their children.

They think the Iraqis will more identify with the thirty-one Christian nations that invaded them, and blew up Baghdad with Shock and Awe, and tortured their sons in Abu Ghraib, than with the furious, armed, insurgent Muslim neighbours and cousins down the street. They think the Palestinians will more identify with the pro-American Fatah crooks who stole all their aid money than with the pious, armed, aggrieved and martyr-minded Hamas they democratically elected to government.

But this is a matter, perhaps, for another book.

Which perhaps I've written already.

231

An estimated amount of tax unpaid by American religions since 1970 is one trillion, three billion, four hundred and fifty-eight million, four hundred and fifty-six thousand dollars. (This assumes twenty-one percent of Americans put in the collection plate or pay for religious publications an average of twenty-two dollars a week, and the average tax avoided is thirty-five percent.)

One trillion, three billion, four hundred and fifty-eight million, four hundred and fifty-six thousand dollars. A sum that could have purchased the entire Amazonian rainforest, given a hundred thousand electric cars by lottery to Chinese motorists and AIDS drugs free for eight years to every infected child in Africa.

Or paid off the debt to China.

But no; taxing religion is wrong.

God needs the money.

He feels it's not his job to create it out of thin air, the way he did the world.

He likes the money.

What else are they going to do with the money?

Give it to the poor?

The poor you always have with you.

We'll see to that.

232

All this would be less disturbing if the larger delusions were confined to America, but this is not so.

Other countries have fallen prey to the virus.

The most unexpected of these, in this millennium anyway, was Iceland.

IN A FARAWAY COUNTRY OF WHICH WE KNOW LITTLE

233

In Iceland the economy was mostly about netting fish. Most able-bodied men would go out in boats, net fish and come home and sell them. In the 1980s the government privatised the fish by introducing quotas dependent on how much each fisherman had caught in the past. One fisherman could sell his quota for a high price to another, or he could borrow money from the bank against his quota to, say, invest or buy a Range Rover.

From 1991 a new Prime Minister, David Oddsson, a poet (poetry being a common pursuit in that sea-dog, storm-washed, saga-maddened nation), declared himself a big fan of Milton Friedman and privatised everything, floated the króna and bade everyone seek wealth adventurously in the free marketplace.

Among those institutions privatised were three banks, the Landsbanki, the Kaupthing and the Glitnir, and fishing. Each man could now have his own licence and net fish to a certain limit, *or sell that licence to a competitor*.

Soon there were fishing multi-millionaires. And their

relatives in the private banks (and everyone's a relative in Iceland, which is among the most inbred of nations) lent them money the private banks borrowed abroad to buy property.

They bought houses, whose value tripled in a year or so, knowing their value was bound to increase throughout eternity, and on this increased value borrowed more money, not in krónas at the local interest rate of 15.5 percent but in other currencies such as the yen at three percent, and made a pile of cash on the currency trade as the króna kept rising.

How could they lose?

With these profits they bought interests in overseas businesses – second-tier airlines, substandard shopping malls, businesses whose value, too, increased.

Soon they were swimming in money, and debt.

What could go wrong?

234

Well, in September of '08 Lehman Brothers collapsed, and so did the króna. It was now worth one-third of what it used to be worth and the young brash adventurous men owed, oh, one hundred thousand dollars on Range Rovers now worth *thirty-five* thousand dollars at the point of sale and one million five hundred thousand dollars on houses worth five hundred thousand dollars at the point of sale.

And the banks, whose assets were those houses, Range Rovers and leverage-borrowed overseas dodgy businesses, collapsed too, and so did the Scottish institutions who had invested money with them, and Russian money (aka 'Moscow Gold') was asked to buy up some of this 'toxic debt', and it was thought that netting fish, a *real* asset, was a better option hereinafter than the endless abstract valuations of debt-mountains that have proved to be made of misty, sunlit, insubstantial Arctic cloud.

And the average debt of every Icelander now (and there are only three hundred thousand of them), man, woman and child, is three hundred and thirty thousand dollars, and the national debt of Iceland eight hundred and fifty percent of its GDP.

And there's no way out but going back to netting fish, which the Harvard-educated second generation feel they are above now, and abolishing the króna, which the floating of caused all the trouble, adopting the euro, and working hard for two thousand years to pay off the debt.

In an excellent, alarming, amusing long article about all this in *Vanity Fair*, now available on the internet, Michael Lewis quotes a bankrupt buinessman saying, 'You have to understand. Iceland is no longer a country. It is a hedge fund.'

235

What made young men think they could run an international finance business with only days or hours of training, and end up ahead of the numbers?

Well, the same thing that made AIG and Goldman Sachs and Lehman Brothers think they could.

They thought the dice were loaded and the game stacked their way. Forever.

And what happened to Lilliput, what happened to Iceland, happened to the Great World.

236

To Enron, for instance.

Its President Jeff Skilling used an accounting trick called 'mark to market' by which the company would list as real profits money that hadn't been earned yet but was thought, or hoped, would be coming in. If the actual profits of last year were ten million he would list for this year fifty million – or whatever figure he chose – as certain income on the company accounts. This confidently asserted untruth (CAU) would push the share price up, and he or other executives would sell off a swag of their shares for tens of millions of dollars. In this way Lou Pai, a Chinese-American Enron executive, cashed in two hundred and fifty million dollars, divorced his wife and moved with his stripper-mistress to Hawaii where he lives now very comfortably.

Yet for most of its decade of glamorous eminence, Enron was losing money. But a divided, semi-psychotic young man called Andy Fastow hid its losses in a round-robin of companies – called JEDI, Jerco, Raptor, LJM and so on – and the *seeming* profits lured JPMorgan Chase, Citibank, Merrill Lynch and the major financial entities of America to – apparently unwittingly, though this is to be doubted – shower Enron with billions.

And so, *while always losing money*, its share price always went up.

'It was a kind of parallel universe,' said Bethany McLean, co-author of *Enron: The Smartest Guys in the Room*, one its executives eventually came to believe in, or *almost* believe in, by a kind of self-hypnosis.

A delusion.

237

The fraud was wonderfully accelerated by political events in California, where 'privatisation' of the electricity grids had lately occurred.

Enron, an energy company, and several accomplice power companies bought up various competing electricity grids, and by contriving power blackouts *forced up the price of their electricity*, whose scarcity was conspired, in a state where hundreds of old people were dying of the heat and air-conditioning was at a premium.

Electricity bills went to the point of pain and President Bush, who had the ability to control prices in America, chose not to, and the Democrat governor Gray Davis was blamed for everything, removed by a constitutional anomaly from office and replaced by Arnold Schwarzenegger.

The more people died, the more the price went up, the more triumphant Enron seemed.

It seemed, while losing billions, to be making bags of money.

The more people died, the more the price went up, the more triumphant Enron seemed.

It seemed, while losing billions, to be making bags of money.

Some of it was to do with the young traders on the floor, who, it was said by a former Enron accountant, were 'out of control'. *We're the future of Enron and we're making half a billion dollars for Enron,* said one, unaware that he was being recorded. *Can you believe that? We'll definitely retire by the time we're thirty.* Another one said to an unseen crony: *We're getting pretty spoiled with all this money. You say you're getting a little scared we're making too much, and I have to agree with you.* And while the temperature went up even higher and wildfires ripped through the hills, the young traders can be heard making calls to shut down the power stations for three or four hours at a time to force the prices up. *Burn, baby, burn!* one of them growled happily.

238

By these and other stratagems, Skilling, his CEO and Chairman Ken Lay and his psychopathic accomplice Fastow (who creamed off forty-five million in pin-money for himself) got the share price up by thirty percent in

1999 and by two hundred percent in 2000, and only when Bethany McLean, then a New York journalist, asked the obvious question, 'How does Enron make its money?' and Skilling accused her of being out to get him did it all begin to unravel, and the emperor be seen to have no clothes.

Eleven billion dollars was lost by various participants or victims of the scam. A long-time employee who had bought stock saw it go in value from three hundred and forty-eight thousand dollars, enough to retire on, to twelve hundred dollars, enough for a bang-up meal for the family and a bullet to the head. Ashamed high-level executive Cliff Baxter committed suicide. Eighty-five thousand people from Arthur Andersen, America's most venerated accounting firm, lost their jobs. All the Enron employees lost theirs too and were given an average of five thousand six hundred dollars in severance pay, and had to leave the building in thirty minutes. Deserted floors with desks, empty chairs, computers and cascading piles of paper gave it a ghostly look in the film that was made of it, *Enron: The Smartest Guys in the Room*.

Fastow got only ten years after agreeing to grass on the rest of them. Lay died of a heart attack at sixty-four while awaiting sentencing. Skilling, the inspirational fantasist, got twenty-four years and four months.

To the end, acquaintances said Lay and Skilling believed that if they kept saying their jumbled arithmetic would all add up somehow, the mystic rescue, the Invisible Hand (IH) would come.

Or no-one would ever find out the eleven billion wasn't there.

The Capitalism Delusion (CD, one might call it). Overvaluing things and borrowing money on their illusory value to risk it elsewhere on bigger and bigger illusions. Squirrelling losses away. Alan Bond did this, and Robert Maxwell, and Conrad Black and Kerry Packer. It's happening all over. The delusion that if you say a number, it will come. And the number will be real, like the ghostly baseballers back from the dead in *Field of Dreams*. *If you build it, they will come.*

How it happens is the question of the month, and the year, and the millennium, and it won't go away.

And, of course, the adjacent question, which is: what are things worth? And how do we agree on this?

239

If a house in Michigan can be worth a dollar, and a loaf of bread in Harare worth 1.6 trillion dollars, and a painting by Van Gogh that *he* sold for four hundred francs be worth around a hundred million dollars by now, what precisely are we playing at?

The substance of things hoped for?

The evidence of things not seen?

240

It is said that Sir Fred Goodwin paid Tony Blair's people four hundred thousand pounds for his knighthood.

It is known that Tony Blair is paid one hundred and sixty thousand pounds an hour for his lecturing.

(It's hard to know what he talks about. 'Get on board with the Americans early,' I guess.)

And Monica Lewinsky ten thousand an hour for hers.

And that Glenda Jackson's frequent nakedness in Oscar-winning films helped make her Minister for Transport in Tony Blair's government. Or that is one theory.

The always-fashionably-clad actress Valerie Hobson, say, would not have got that far in politics.

Especially after it was found that her husband, John Profumo, the then Minister for War, dallied with whores and may have passed on national security secrets to one of them, who was also 'seeing' a Russian spy.

Valerie Hobson stood by her husband and got no films after that. Her career was finished.

This is in contrast to Jodie Foster for whose love John Hinckley Jnr shot Ronald Reagan in the chest.

Her value went up after that, and she won two Oscars, and it went up even more.

As did the value, naked or not, of Princess Diana after she went on television and denounced the British heir to the throne. 'There were three of us in this marriage,' she said, 'so it was a bit crowded.'

And more so after she was killed.

And Russell Crowe's value to a Hollywood picture went down (and he has not been a true star lead since then) after he flung a phone at a hotel clerk in New York and was taken away in handcuffs.

Forgive me for raising these matters but they seem to suggest that the prefix 'sir' or eleven blow-jobs or a recognisable name or a viewed blonde pubis or certain sexual acts with lower-class girls, a flung phone, an attempted assassination and a death in a car crash have a large market value, depending on the economic cycle, a market value as house prices and currencies do.

And this substance of things hoped for, this evidence of things not seen, is expressed in money.

241

Which means market values are unstable, and a free market not to be trusted, and a *global* free market even more unstable and untrustworthy.

And it should be regulated; discuss.

Does anybody doubt this now?

THE HABIT OF WORK

242

These things may have been remarked on before but one thing that has not been is the value to the economy of work that is *enjoyable*.

There used to be a lot of this about.

You could earn a comfortable wage, enough to buy a house with a lawn and raise five children, teaching Latin. Or tutoring in Ancient History and going on digs to Herculaneum and holidays to Venice and Jerusalem. You could ride a bicycle through clean country air delivering telegrams at fourteen years of age, or newspapers at eight years of age, accruing a little money to buy comics with and learning the work ethic, the habit of work.

You could drive an elevator in a big department store or announce on a loudspeaker the day's bargains, crafting your acting skills. You could act in radio dramas, receiving the scripts just minutes before you played Winston Smith in *Nineteen Eighty-Four*, or Carl Phillips in *War of the Worlds*. You could adapt for radio the world's classics, as Howard Koch, who later adapted *Casablanca*, did for Orson

Welles' Mercury Theatre. You could write film criticism or review new books, in the dozens of little magazines or suburban newspapers competing for your attention in any provincial capital. In Chicago, for instance, there was the *Chicago Sun-Times*, *Chicago Tribune*, *Daily Herald*, *Chicago Daily News*, *Today*, *Chicago Defender*, *Chicago Reader*, *The SouthtownStar*, the *Daily Southtown*, *News Sun*, *Newsweek* and *Life*, in Manchester the *Manchester Evening News*, *Horse and Hound*, *The Guardian*, *South Manchester Reporter*, *News of the World*, *The Times*, *Woman*, the *Daily Telegraph*, *The Economist* and *Woman's Weekly*, in Sydney the *Sunday Review*, the *National Times*, the *Sunday Australian*, *The Nation*, the *King's Cross Weekly*, *Man Magazine*, *Women's Weekly*, *New Idea*, *Pol*, *Chance*, *Dolly*, the *North Shore Times*, the *Daily Telegraph*, *The Sun*, the *Daily Mirror*, the *Sun Herald*, the *Sunday Telegraph*, the *Sydney Morning Herald*, the *Manly Daily* and the *Wentworth Courier*, all competing for vigorous, literate readership in 1972.

You could work on the railways, as the author did, in the summer vacation while completing university. You could work for a while as a bus conductor, or a tram conductor, perfecting your English and picking up girls. You could be, illegally, a bookie's runner or a nude model for photography courses or a sidewalk artist duplicating Michelangelo's *Creation of Adam* in coloured chalks on a concrete footpath, soon to be washed away. You could type up students' handwritten theses or deliver, enjoyably, on a motorbike small packages from suburb to suburb while studying Ancient History at night at the university. Or you collected tolls on the Harbour Bridge and said hello to motorists you recognised.

243

Now nearly all these agreeable jobs are gone. And the best ones still recruiting are in call centres where you bully twenty luckless debtors an hour for money they haven't got or lose your position for not working hard enough. Or you work for a medical insurance firm telling people they're going to die, sorry about that, because their 'pre-existing condition' disqualifies them for the money they need for invasive, expensive, life-saving treatment.

Or for the army as a recruiter telling jobless slumside youth – who would have been telegram boys in the days of telegrams – that a year in Iraq as part of the Surge won't be so bad, and they'll get to go to college if they survive. Or for the Church of Scientology approaching depressed young men in pedestrian tunnels and asking them if they feel their true worth is going unrecognised in a busy heartless world, and saying they can change all that, they can enlarge their life as Tom Cruise did, if they will only walk up these stairs and sign up and hand over their family money to this matchless, golden, eleven-step pathway to personal fulfilment.

Or cleaning public lavatories. Or mopping up after

shotgun suicides (as the girls do in *Sunshine Cleaning*). Or guarding big buildings all night, looking in on the offices of men who earn eight million a year. Or delivering hundreds of thousands of dollars, daily, to ATMs, wondering where it all came from and what harm it would do to snaffle a bit of it now and then. Or cleaning the honeymoon suites of costly hotels, wondering if the luxury orgy of the rock stars there last night was as drug-fuelled, sexy and enjoyable as the night porter said.

Or maybe doing two of the above sorts of jobs each day, to keep up the mortgage on a flat you can't sell any more for even half the price you paid for it.

244

So it isn't good any more, the way it was for the author in his twenties in the not-so-far-off days when you could quit a job and travel overseas for a year and come back on a Thursday and have another job on the Monday week.

You have to stay in the job that's available now, and it's terrible.

And what you do is take designer drugs on the weekend and seek empty sex – and sometimes find it – and wonder why your self-worth is so down in the dumps and if the Scientologists may be right after all, maybe there is a way. Or you go to the pub and watch football and punch somebody and end up with a bleeding eyeball or a broken arm in hospital with cops asking gently who was in the wrong.

Is this lack of good jobs, though, and this abundance of lousy jobs, good for the economy?

Doesn't this mechanisation of delivery services and the downsizing of academia (fewer classes, fewer extracurricular activities, fewer history courses, more emphasis on management and financial services skills) serve the economy over all, put up the average citizen's average income, make him able to pay the higher mortgages and rents that come, alas, in train with it?

Well, no, not really.

Not really.

245

I'll tell you why I say 'not really', old friend.

It's because so many urban workers, aghast at the work they're doing, the cruelty of it, the nastiness of it, the distress of it, the hours, the nights, the weeks, spend a lot of their money *illegally* on designer drugs or hash or smack or smacked-out prostitutes, and the money vanishes out of the economy into the black economy, the illegal economy, which pays no taxes and goes overseas. About 1.4 billion Australian dollars, for instance, goes overseas each year to heroin traders running opium resin from, mainly, Afghanistan and Burma. And that's a pity.

Some might even call it a criminal waste.

And the culture of illegality grows and spreads, for instance, into the downloading of music young people listen to while taking drugs and the consequent impover-ishment of musicians. And the growth of gambling, and the drowning out by the noise of poker machines of good musicians. And so on. And the honest economy makes less and less money, pays less and less in tax for public hospitals, safe trains, safe highways. And the whole thing runs down. And that's a pity.

If the jobs were better, as they used to be, the society would be better too. And happier.

And the economy easier to get along in.

246

It's not as if the changes, not all of them, make practical sense either. The loss to young men of the jobs they once had as bus conductors, for instance, has not only drawn the young men towards drugs and crime and cost the economy a packet *that* way, it's also been shown to make no sense financially as well.

On the bus the author takes from central Sydney to Palm Beach, for instance, a journey of seventy-five minutes, there are many stops, no bus conductor and many testing delays while queuing Japanese tourists ask the driver if he takes Visa.

There is also a queue for a machine where bits of radiated plastic bought in newsagents at hours convenient to newsagents are inserted and read electronically.

All this takes, at my stop, about three minutes and

would have taken, if there had been a conductor, thirty seconds. To get people on to the bus in these technologically advanced times takes three more minutes than it would have if there had been a young male teenage conductor with a hand-wound ticket-dispensing device and a jingly leather bag to put the money in.

To make up for the lack of a conductor, moreover, also on the bus is what amounts to a television studio, which transmits many images of a number of seats at the back of the bus to the front of the bus – of, for instance, me seen back on, raising my hand, three seconds after I have done so.

This prevents people from behaving badly on the bus, something the teenage conductor could have done, with a quiet word and a raised fist, much more cheaply.

The teenage conductor would have cost the nation thirty thousand dollars a year.

The technological juggernaut that is now this bus, with its two sets of ticket machines, the three television cameras, the television screen and the downtown computer to keep it all going, costs, say, seven times that amount.

And the bus *still takes longer* and thus encumbered loses three runs a day, one thousand and ninety-five runs a year, and puts more pressure on the multiply-embattled bus driver who retires early or maybe crashes the bus.

Because there is no conductor on the bus, women don't like to travel on it after eight p.m. This costs the bus company money too. And the young migrant men who otherwise might have found gainful work, *and the habit of work*, and broadened the scope of their minds and found a wife, sometimes go into crime instead, and cost us fifty-six thousand dollars a year each for their incarceration.

It would have saved us, on average, eighteen million dollars a year to have kept these conductors dispensing tickets out of their medieval clockwork device, and putting money in their leather bag.

But no, no, we can't do that, we have to put these people in call centres, and more and more machines on the bus.

Even if the machines cost seven times as much as the people.

247

This preference for robots over people, this instinctive punishment of young people for merely existing and wanting to have fun, is a religious impulse that lures away the economic fundamentalists from simple arithmetic into quasi-fascist theology.

Of *course* it is better to put people out of work and machines in their places, even if the people are cheaper and save lives. It is a matter of principle, a moral imperative. Down with people! Bring on the robots! The slaves!

I swear the following conversation took place in Bathurst, a big regional town in Australia.

I had arrived on the bus at nine-thirty p.m., found no restaurants open, was hungry and booked into my motel.

I noticed that a Pizza Palace was half a mile down the street and it was open. I wondered if they delivered or if I could pre-book an order and walk there.

I rang the number in the book.

'Pizza Palace,' said a precise male voice.

'Hello,' I said, 'I'd like to order a large pizza, half margarita, half vegetarian, and I was wondering if you—'

'What is the date of your birth, sir?'

'Pardon?'

'The date of your birth.'

'Why is that relevant?'

'Our company is doing a customer survey of dietary tendencies—'

'Yes, yes, 10th May, 1942. Do you deliver?'

'What Pizza Palace are you calling, sir?'

'Yours. The Pizza Palace on William Street, Bathurst.'

'Bathurst, Australia?'

The penny began to drop.

'Yes,' I said. 'That's the one.'

'I do not think we have a Pizza Palace in Bathurst, Australia, sir.'

'Nonsense, I can see it through my window. It's half a mile away.'

'Oh yes, you are right, here it is.'

'What country are you in?'

'I am in Mumbai.'

'Do they train you in Australian slang expressions?'

'I am not at liberty to give that information, sir. A half margarita and a vegetarian, is it, sir?'

'Yes it is. Will you deliver?'

'I have not been apprised of our policy on that in Bathurst, Australia.'

'Why don't you go then and ask?'

'It is not our policy to seek to influence local outlets in this area of policy, sir.'

'Are you a university graduate?'

'I have an MA and MBA, sir, from the University of Calcutta.'

'Not enough work for MBAs?'

'Not currently, sir, not in my part of the world.'

'So I have to walk there.'

'I would say so, sir.'

'In the time it has taken to have this conversation with you I could have walked there, ordered, eaten and begun the walk back.'

'You are exaggerating, I think, sir.'

'Exaggerating, am I? Right. Please cancel the order.'

'Very good, sir. What is your home postcode? It is for the survey.'

'May you and your employers and the global market never have a day's luck,' I said.

And I hung up, and feared a moment later I had done the wrong thing.

Poor devil, I thought, poor devil.

248

It's possible this loss of my custom forever can be justified by the global Pizza Palace chain in some way that makes *economic* sense, but the arithmetical sense of it eludes me.

It would have been easier for the people down the road to answer the phone and cook me a pizza, which I would have walked down the road, in fairly good humour, and eaten and paid for, leaving a tip.

But this is the fashion of the times. Work for young people in prosperous countries is forbidden, and it must go where it can, to cash-strapped university graduates in poorer countries.

You get a ten-cent cheaper pizza that way.

And a serial killer who might be more gainfully employed bringing pizza to my motel on a motorbike.

You know it makes sense.

249

Did I eat that night? Oh yes. I walked a mile to Domino's, which was still open, ate a really filthy pizza there and walked back, cursing the Subcontinent, to bed at midnight and slept little.

Which brings me to the crux, the nub of the argument against global economics . . .

. . . which is that jobs go overseas (call-centre jobs for instance, aircraft mechanic jobs for instance) and hedge funds can go overseas and CEOs like Sol Trujillo, global capitalist, but people can't. If they try to, their boats are turned back and they drown off Gibraltar.

Or the Australian navy looks the other way while three hundred and fifty-three of them drown in the Arafura Sea.

Or they die of thirst in the deserts north of the Rio Grande, or are turned into fearful slaves by the people smugglers who take them in refrigerator trucks to the meat works of Washington State.

Or they're turned back by armed guards when they try to cross from Gaza into Egypt. Or they're frozen to death in panel vans on their way from China to England.

How can global economics be global if money can move, and products, and armaments, and cluster-bombs across borders and oceans and *people can't*?

How come we can't protect ourselves from invading products, but we *can* protect ourselves from people?

The answer that people thieve jobs and products don't is rubbish.

Because cheap T-shirts do. And cheap foreign cars do.

Or am I wrong?

250

Can a level playing field be level if a billion people aren't even let *near* it, let alone onto it?

How can it *be* a level playing field if it has a fence around it?

251

Can a global system that protects itself from five hundred million hungry, hard-working, potential immigrants be global still?

Or is it a Big Lie, as great as the threat to Aryan maidenhood by the lustful, groping, diseased and greedy Jews?

252

Repeating that point.

How can it *be* a level playing field if there's a fence around it?

How can it *be* a level playing field if people drown swimming towards it?

253

If global economics were truly global it would include the eight hundred million Muslims who don't believe in lending money. And believe that American capitalism is the pawn of Satan.

Do we include them in, or do we include them out?

254

No, the truth of it is that, like Italian fascist corporatism, it exalts the few and doesn't let the many – that is most of the world – anywhere near the crumbs that trickle down from the rich man's table.

I repeat, if we can't let in people that threaten jobs,

how can we let in products that threaten jobs, and keep abolishing jobs, a thousand since you started reading this chapter?

255

'Empire is a *racket*,' George Orwell once said, 'and there's no other way to describe it.' And global economics, he might have added if he'd lived now, is only Empire by another name.

It's by making easy the movement of goods, and making hard the movement of people, that empires work. While India was being gouged of its wealth – for two hundred years – no Indians were allowed to settle in England. No Africans either. Nor West Indians, nor Chinese. The point was to keep them out, as it is today, lest they undermine with their cheap labour the standard of living of their exploiters. Standards of living that were built up by exploiting them. Cockneys with Indian servants in India came to like the imperial lifestyle, and married one of them, maybe, and had golden children with her, and 'stayed on'.

256

Global economics is a racket; discuss.

Economic fundamentalism is a crime against humanity; discuss.

It keeps AIDS drugs from needy African children; discuss.

It says its 'intellectual property' in these drugs is more important that these children's lives; discuss.

And it pays its CEOs, oh, thirty-eight dollars a minute for deciding these things; discuss.

257

While the author was writing this chapter the Summit of the Americas took place.

And President Barack Obama, who had agreed that Cubans resident in Florida could visit their relatives in Cuba and send them money, was greeted civilly by Hugo Chávez, the democratically elected 'dictator' of Venezuela. And Hillary Clinton was greeted civilly that same week by Raúl Castro, who said 'some reforms' like freedom of the press and multi-party elections were now 'on the table' if America let its citizens come directly to Cuba as tourists and spend money there. And we may yet see Obama and Fidel, the heroes of two different sorts of American life, in a clasped, smiling handshake before long.

And diplomatic ties, which were no problem with Perón's Argentina, or Pinochet's Chile, or Marcos's the Philippines, or Suharto's Indonesia, or Mao's China, or Stalin's Russia, or Hitler's Germany for that matter, will be re-established after forty-eight years of trade war.

'What has Cuba ever done to hurt America?' Fidel once asked. 'Name one thing.'

And silence followed.

258

There was one thing, of course. Cuba had won a small war at the Bay of Pigs against the CIA, a few hundred Batista nostalgics and some Mafia gambling barons whom Che and Fidel had put to flight – economic fundamentalists, you might call them – and so wounded America's pride that the Castros were never forgiven.

Insult its Mafias' pride, and America becomes a tiger.

Prove that I lie.

259

This book pretty much began with Cuba, and this part of it might end here.

Remember that the Castros never made any crooked money out of Cuba, never squirrelled away in a Swiss bank billions of dollars as other dictators (and the Mafia) have done. And that they haven't dealt in drugs or prostitutes. And that Fidel came to his senses on the Beatles and eventually unveiled a statue of John Lennon sitting on a park bench in Vedado, Havana, and spoke in praise of his music, and said in a press conference afterwards that the ban on it was 'a bureaucratic mistake, and nothing to do with me'.

And so it went.

THE ONLY WAY TO FLY

260

So much of what happens in what we must call a 'capitalist democracy' derives from confident public assertions of unexamined hypotheses (CPAUH).

And many, many of these have the ideas 'free' or 'freedom' in them.

'Free trade', as we have seen, involves, in some regions, not all, the freedom to enslave. And slavery is not freedom.

While writing this paragraph I saw the consummate author and politician Barack Obama, in a press conference in Mexico, refer to the idea of 'freedom of speech and religion'.

This is a foolish confluence of concepts. Because religion *of its very nature* opposes itself to freedom of speech.

A Christian is not allowed to joke about Jesus. A Muslim is not allowed to joke about Mahomet. If he does he may be killed, as Salman Rushdie's translator was, and several threatened Danish cartoonists feared they might be, when they portrayed Mahomet's turban as a tight-fitting bomb.

Freedom of religion is not freedom of speech. The two ideas are miles apart; the one precludes the other.

And freedom of speech has nothing to do with Rupert Murdoch, who owns one hundred and eighty newspapers and many, many television and cinema outlets, because he himself does not believe in it.

Unless his one hundred and eighty editors agree with him, and they do, and agree with him in particular detail, they cannot keep their jobs, nor can his reporters and broadcasters. Roger Ailes, the CEO of Fox News (thirty-seven dollars eighty-six cents a minute) decides in collaboration with Murdoch what is the catchphrase of the day and loyally, in unison, his broadcasters parrot it, Bill O'Reilly 'the no-spin zone' among them.

261

In Rupert, I believe, is further evidence that globalism and a free democracy cannot long coexist, and every year that 'global free trade' continues, democratic freedoms diminish.

The attack on the Twin Towers, an event so global that George Bush didn't know who to declare war on for a while, caused the Patriot Act, and the US government's right to lock up a suspect for the rest of his life and not bring him to trial if, under torture – and certain forms of torture were specifically allowed – he did not 'freely' confess to terrorism.

And he could be locked up too for *thinking* about terrorism, committing in Orwell's crisp neologism Thoughtcrime, for intending to do something bad in the future.

This is a long, long way from freedom of speech, and the world's premier global-free-trader, America, brought it in and Rupert Murdoch applauded it.

I have elsewhere listed what Rupert Murdoch believes, and what his reporters and editors and broadcasters and editorial writers are obliged to believe, or say they believe, their own freedom of speech being one such false assertion.

In a global enterprise like News Limited, in a global enterprise like the War on Terror, or a global enterprise like the Third Reich, there is no such thing as freedom of speech.

From the days of the Roman Empire, globalism and freedom have been opposing concepts. And they remain so today.

Rome toyed with democracy for a century or so. But when it gained an Empire, it opted for Dictatorship – or what might be called the Unified Aristocratic Precedence Principle (UAPP) – and it held to that high ideal for five hundred years; discuss.

It was as if the Bush family had taken over the Presidency and their descendants ruled America, and a good deal of the known world, till 2500.

Which some say was their plan.

262

Tightly bound up with globalist capitalism is Advertising.

It is a curious pursuit, whose purpose, it is said, is to provide 'additional information which might persuade a potential customer to prefer our product to another'. That *I dreamed I raced with the wind in my Maidenform bra,* and so on.

In many cases, it is a pack of lies. Toothpastes said to 'provide round-the-clock protection from tooth decay' do not. Cars said to be safe because they provide 'power when you need it' are speed-traps likely to tempt you to risk early death. Pills that are said to ease your anxieties can give you waking nightmares and drive you to suicide.

In *Mad Men* we see what advertising executives used to be like: chain-smoking, adulterous, self-loathing, given to three-martini lunches and a whisky-and-ice for morning tea, fighting like muskrats for the Lucky Strike account and the right to lure teenagers into a life of cigarettes and cancerous death which *they knew was on the cards as early as 1950.* Suppressing evidence of that cancer, fabricating studies of their own, as good professionals would.

Advertising is the natural propaganda arm of global capitalism – persuading the Third World that Coke, an engine of diabetes, improves your mood. Or that Nestlé's powdered milk is good for your suckling baby, though they sometimes die of the knock-on effects of it.

It kills a lot of people, as its sponsor global capitalism

does. But perhaps the worst thing it does is take fortunes out of the pockets of its customers.

Each thirty-second ad during *Desperate Housewives* in America now costs three hundred and ninety-four thousand dollars. If five of those ads run that night it costs their customers, to whom the cost is passed on, one million nine hundred and seventy thousand dollars – for just that one night.

On top of this is the cost of making the ad, which may be around a million dollars.

It's a kind of tariff, really. A tariff you pay to ensure your product arrives in the shop.

Advertising is a hidden tax; a hidden GST; a hidden punishment for purchase; discuss.

263

Like most capitalist activity, it is anti-competition. Small manufacturers of good products are squeezed out of the market by loud, bright, bustling juggernauts of advertising for inferior products. And fewer good things are made, or sold. And clever men and women go bankrupt.

And this is the way things have to be.

There is no alternative.

Can a system with so many lies intertwined in it be a good one? Discuss.

Or is it a system like fascism: corrupt, untruthful and brutal at its heart?

264

Do people act in their own self-interest when they buy a car for their teenage son, who has not yet the ability to imagine his own mortality, and contribute with its pollution to the end of the world, or not?

Seems not.

Car-owning, like tobacco-inhaling, is a sometimes lethal addiction, funded by governments all over the world, and people suicidally embrace it, as certain Niugini native people do annual tribal wars.

And one hundred and sixteen drivers and their potential earnings are wiped out in the US alone every day.

265

In a great work of theatre, *Lipsynch*, script-managed and directed by Robert Lepage, the most significant actor-manager since Shakespeare, the audience for eight hours follows the workings of the capitalist, global world.

It begins with a crying baby on an aeroplane flying from Hamburg to New York. The baby's mother, a young woman, has died of unknown causes and a woman in a nearby seat, a famous opera singer, takes and holds the baby and, after a while, determines to adopt him.

The baby grows up to be a professional composer, and then a film director, and determines to make a film about his unknown mother, who was apparently a Nicaraguan babysitter working for a Hamburg professor she was in love with, who was killed in an accident.

He moves the story in time to World War II and the Holocaust and in fairly funny circumstances, involving hectic superstars, he shoots it in Italy. The film is a touch sentimental, but well received.

His adoptive mother the opera singer then tells him what really happened. His real mother was a seventeen-year-old Nicaraguan waitress orphaned when her activist parents were killed by the Somoza dictatorship during an Ortega uprising (Ortega is once again the duly-elected Prime Minister of Nicaragua) and sold by her uncle for five hundred dollars to a Hamburg pimp, who finds her virginity attractive and tells her he is a professor and she will be his assistant in Hamburg, takes her there, has her gang-raped and addicted to heroin, and convinces her she owes him money which she can only pay off by unceasing, round-the-clock prostitution.

When the pimp is killed in a motorbike accident she escapes into a hippie commune, discovers she is pregnant, has the baby and borrows enough money to fly back to Nicaragua and to her uncle, whom she still trusts, but she dies of her weakened, addicted condition on the plane.

At the end of the play she is reunited, as a ghost, with the son she never knew and the woman who raised him in her stead.

It is one of the greatest experiences people who see it have ever had, and this includes the author.

This is so in part because it portrays without flinching the true unacceptable, merciless face of the globalist world.

The traffic in young women. The easy availability of drugs. The usefulness of addiction to the capitalist process. The ability some people have to shut down their sympathy and do irreparable harm to those who have come to trust them. The market value of a maidenhead. The expendable, innocent people of the Third World.

Is there any possibility of 'the human face of capitalism' in this, the world it has created?

I don't think so.

How about you?

266

In Bhutan, an absolute monarchy, the absolute monarch Jigme Singye Wangchuck a while back decreed there should be a new economic measurement called Gross National Happiness (GNH).

In pursuit of this goal tobacco was banned, and billboards, and plastic bags, because it was thought they made the country 'less happy'.

Though it meant some citizens were by some measurements 'poor' in comparison with westerners, it was thought this was okay with most of them.

Coke and Pepsi hoardings were pulled down because, as Jigme Thinley, the Minister for Culture, told a BBC reporter, he wasn't sure that Bhutan's children *needed* to consume Coke and Pepsi since they had such fresh water there, not bottled but free-flowing. Why was it, he asked himself, that we, as parents, were allowing our children, and even ourselves, to be beguiled, to be deluded, by the force of these hoardings and by what appeared on television. Why were we doing this?

Television came in 1999 with forty-six channels very suddenly and, as happened elsewhere in other cultures, children neglected their homework, families ceased talking over dinner, less reading was done and one grandmother at least neglected her prayers and stopped cooking. So it was thought wise to ban some of the more popular programmes, like, say, 'World Wrestling' but to keep the local news and the Discovery Channel.

They put in one set of traffic lights at one point, but the people found them 'unsatisfactory' and the traffic cop was restored.

Sometimes we wonder, Mr Thinley went on, when we look at the industrialised world and at the developing world, if there has been any advancement in terms of civilisation or if in fact there has been a *de-civilisation*, since civilisation has to do with development of the human individual, the mind, the finer aspects of humanity, and those seem to him to have been lost.

One also wondered, he said, why Bhutan happened to be the first to be thinking about such a process when happiness was really the ultimate desire of every human individual. Why was it that no other country had used this as the basis for policy, for programmes or for resource allocation?

'In a way, we in Bhutan are pioneers and it is sad that we should find ourselves to be so. We should actually be in company with the rest of the world.'

It seems not a bad way of looking at things, if you believe (as I do) that there are alternatives.

Communism looked that way too, for a while.

FROM EACH ACCORDING
TO HIS CAPACITY

267

Communism became unpopular not because of its kindly redistributionist theory of 'from each according to his capacity and to each according to his need' or its occasional crop failures, but because of some bad men who ran it and the bad deeds ordinary people remembered them for.

Stalin's gulags, his slaughter of the Kulaks, the show trials of his revolutionary comrades and their subsequent executions by firing squad, his sacrifice of twenty million Russians to a war he might have won more easily had he not murdered his better army generals before it started and harried their successors with idiotic battle strategies and his needless execution of surviving Russians who might, he suspected, have been corrupted in German prison camps by anti-communist ideals; all these things and the adjacent tyrannies of Gomulka, Hoxha, Chervenkov, Rákosi and Mao gave Communism a bad name.

He was a troubled and dangerous, probably paranoid man. And though an avid reader of world literature (in his library are notes on almost every page of Austen, Dickens, Tolstoy, Shakespeare, Orwell, Plutarch, Priestley, Jack London and so on) he ordered terrible retributive acts that soiled and corroded the name of communism forever.

A similar soiling and corrosion is happening lately to capitalism; discuss.

268

Its deeds in South America; its hounding and murder of Che Guevara; its overthrowing of Salvador Allende; its corrupt election of George W. Bush; its falsehood-based invasion and smashing-up of Iraq; its failure to stop the genocide in Rwanda and Darfur and the merciless slaying of children in Gaza; its corrupt embrace of Putin and the neo-communist moguls of Red China; its censorship of the dreadful news of global warming and its opposition to methods of energy production that might have saved a planet now gravely damaged and possibly doomed; all these greedy neglectful practices bespeak a system, and the kind of nasty, selfish men who run it, that has reached its use-by date and should be wound up.

And replaced.

Prove that I lie.

269

It only took one Stalin to wreck world communism. The Dubceks, Kruschevs, Gorbachevs, Guevaras, Trotskys,

Titos, Ho Chi Minhs and Deng Xiaopings, who mitigated its more evil tendencies and on the whole meant well, proved useless against the propaganda tsunami that Stalin provided, as useless as the slogan 'Hindenburg – the only way to fly'.

And so it is with the deeds of Lay and Madoff, Bush and Cheney, Bond and Black and Goldsmith and Murdoch and Skilling in the years since the Berlin Wall came down and jackal capitalism, unleashed, went roving and sniffing around the globe.

Capitalism is a system that has begun to stink; discuss.

It is rotting and will soon disappear, like paranoid Stalinist cruelty; discuss.

And so it goes.

270

And that's about it, really. Is there anything more one should say?

Anything at all?

Oh, yes.

WHAT IS TO BE DONE?

271

To sum up what we have agreed on, thus far:

We have seen that capitalism is a merciless, mindless delusion and those greedy fools who run it are beyond redemption from their remorseless, habitual insanity. We have seen that it has much in common with terrorism and piracy but is not so small-time. We have seen that like Empire and slavery it has shattered thus far perhaps a billion lives. We have seen it is monstrously unfair and rewards the cruellest among us while punishing the decent, community-minded, child-rearing majority.

But what is to be done about it?

What can be managed while it still has, to a great extent, its foot on our throat?

How can we make things better?

What, old friend, is to be done?

272

We could ask for an apology and a public act of harakiri by Ben Bernanke and Hank Paulson with Japanese swords before Congress for getting the big numbers wrong when it counted. We could arrest and try for 'lethal ignorance' (LI) the hundred top executives of Standard & Poor's who gave a tick to the profit projections of Lehman Brothers and AIG, and sentence those found guilty to a lethal injection or eight hundred years in prison, the outcome to be decided by a toss of a coin or, as it is better known, the Invisible Hand.

We could pass retrospective legislation and hang, draw and quarter any CEO found responsible for ten deaths by industrial pollution or avoidable industrial accident.

We could round up every economist who was found to be still preaching the same nonsense in November, 2008, and lock them up naked for twenty years in small, bright rooms with constant replays of Glenn Beck and Bill O'Reilly and Tammy Wynette at deafening volume bullying every second of their wakeful, howling, pleading prison sentence into eventual insanity.

But we probably shouldn't. We probably shouldn't be vengeful, punishing or cruel, the way they were. We should probably acknowledge that the gentle Obama will want a milder retribution and is skilful enough to devise one.

We should probably look instead, alas, at *future policy*, and the limits of the world in which we must make it work.

273

A world in which, for instance, protectionism is coming back.

(Not that it ever went away. Ask any rich Ohio farmer paid by the US government to burn his crops, or sell them at bargain-basement prices overseas.)

And we have to find moral reasons for bringing it back.

274

We could say, for instance, that China is an evil place, they have public executions there and cut up the condemned men's corpses into body parts they then sell to Hong Kong millionaires, and *because of this* we're putting a two hundred percent tariff on all their exported clothing.

This might allow us to revive our own clothing industry and some of the country towns it flourished in.

We really should have a clothing industry, whatever country we live in.

A clothing industry gives a lot of work to teenage girls and part-time work to young mothers. It provides young women (and some young men) with artistic possibilities as designers. It adds to cultural pride and the various cowboy hats, embroidered shirts, designer jeans and woollen sweaters that bespeak a region.

There is no downside to a clothing industry whose workers are well paid. The argument that those country-town people sacked from it can 'find work in other sectors of the economy' is idiotic.

If there's an argument for having no clothing industry, no clothing industry at all, plus no boot-making industry at all, and no hat-making industry at all, and the argument is that wage slaves and child slaves in other cultures do it more *efficiently*, and though slavery is wrong we should go along with it, *in order to not have a clothing industry*, and let the Chinese have one, where is the sense in it? How does it all add up?

Please explain.

275

The economic fundamentalists believe there should be no tariffs on anything. That protecting local industries is wrong.

Which is pretty much like saying we should take no precautions to protect ourselves from swine flu.

In economics, as in swine flu, let the fittest survive.

The progressive abolition of tariffs is proven madness.

We bring the tariffs on imported cars down from fifty-seven percent to ten percent, and many thousands of Australian car workers lose their jobs.

We bring the tariffs down to five percent, and many more car workers lose their jobs.

And this is good, the economic fundamentalists say. This is part of the process. The sacked, disrupted, frightened workers will move to 'another sector of the economy'. One that hasn't been mechanised yet and has vacancies.

Really?

What sector of the economy is that?

276

We have to revive the nineteenth-century idea that nations have national interests, and the biggest national interest of a nation is jobs for its people, and the money they make from the jobs and spend on each other.

And it's in a nation's national interest to protect itself with tariffs. As nations throughout history always have.

277

The question then arises, and it's a big one but not a hard one, of how high or low the tariffs should be.

It's not a hard one because you only have to look back at a time when they worked best.

In Australia, for instance, or this is the author's view, they worked best in 1988.

In 1988, the tariff on imported cotton was 40 percent; imported wool 40 percent; imported tractors and motorcars 25 percent; golf clubs and tennis balls 25 percent; zips, buttons, biros and fountain pens 20 percent; nuclear reactors 15 percent; juice extractors and toasters 35 percent; dolls 20 percent; tobacco products 15 percent; Carrera marble 15 percent; zinc, copper and aluminium

15 percent; paints and varnishes 15 percent; writing ink and lipstick 20 percent; fireworks 20 percent; 16mm film 15 percent; cane sugar 15 percent; pasta 10 percent; preserved gherkins and olives 10 percent; wine 11 percent. You get the idea.

In 1988, we still had a clothing industry and an auto industry, we still made our own Arnott's biscuits and Berlei bras and Cottee's jam and Bonds underpants.

What would be wrong with those tariff levels now?

Would they help, or hurt?

278

China wouldn't buy our coal any more, is what would be wrong. Or buy less of it. Or so we are told.

And that would cost us, maybe, thirty thousand jobs.

It almost certainly would.

And the tariffs would bring back – eventually – two hundred and fifty thousand jobs.

279

Saying this isn't so is like saying the protection America gives to its farmers isn't helpful to farm workers, and the protection Japan gives to its rice farms isn't helpful to its rice workers.

How does that add up?

It doesn't, and it never has. It is a Confidently Asserted Untruth (CAU) and the world, like a fool, believed it.

It will mean that foreign luxury goods, big-screen televisions, fine wines, rare cheeses and luxury imported clothes will be more expensive. They certainly will.

But it will mean there will be more people in work and able to buy them.

280

It might be valuable to state here the guiding principle of this book.

This is that economics is not and should not be about the sale of tangible goods, it is about the supply of money to humans.

Let me repeat that. It is about the supply of money to humans.

This is not too hard to decipher as an economic theory.

281

For many, many of the goods an economy sells to a customer are not tangible.

Scientology, for instance, gives its customers no tangible product. Nor does psychoanalysis. In each case a better life is promised, and credit taken for however you feel after treatment. And a lot of money changes hands.

This is true too of the many branches of the Christian religion, which promise you eternal felicity in endless green fields and a crystal city and cuddlesome lions and lambs and endless hellfire for your heathen enemies but supplies no *photographs* of these things nor evidentiary testimony from those who have been there.

And a lot of money goes into church collection plates, or pays for lavishly illustrated books and annotated Bibles and the wages of gospel ministers, choirmasters, the ruling professors of religious universities and the headmasters of sectarian schools and the travel expenses of Mormon missionaries roving the known world to sell a product that is not *tangible*, a product for which there is no *hard evidence*, a product that you are asked to take on faith.

The substance of things hoped for, the evidence of things not seen.

And a lot of money changes hands.

Whose value we take on faith.

282

The substance of things hoped for, the evidence of things not seen.

Which is the way the life insurance business works too, on the promise that there are sheaves of money at the end of the tunnel, and AIG or HIH or Lehman Brothers won't go broke in the meantime. And the way the futures business works, that gold or pork bellies will be up in value when you need them to be.

Or that the disease you get is the one you've insured for, and not one of the five hundred others.

Which is, as we have lately seen, and Michael Moore has shown, a delusion.

This is true of the world's fastest-growing industry, Security, whose intangible product is a leader who is *not* assassinated, a skyscraper *not* burgled, a cash-conveying van *not* robbed.

The substance of things hoped for, the evidence of things not seen. Coming to a street near you at five times the price it was ten years ago.

With more security cameras than you can shake a stick at, photographing ordinary irrelevant arrivals and departures of ordinary innocent people, on the off-chance that they might be bogeymen.

283

Possibly half the US economy works on products that are not there, the SDI (Star Wars), for instance, *which will never be completed, though one hundred billion dollars has been spent on it,* or the twenty thousand three hundred and thirty-five nuclear weapons stacked up that will never be used.

So much of the economy works on intangibles or rumours, or insubstantial things like stardom and song and a sunny weekend for the rock festival and no rain on the parade, or the future appeal of a nose-job or a bum-lift or the nostalgic appeal of a street once frequented by the Beatles, or Mahomet, or Ramses II, that it's fair to say that the currently prevailing idea that you have to have tangible products (mined coal, portable radios, penicillin, Viagra, colour magazines, biros) to have an economy is just plain wrong.

You can have, as the Catholic Church shows, a product as illusory, as delusional as a virgin with children, an immortal, unpenetrated, caring, cock-teasing woman nobody's lately met, and *still make money out of it.*

Which means you can have an economy, or a big sector of an economy, without a tangible product.

But you can't, you really can't, my dear old friend, have an economy without people.

284

Economic fundamentalism wonderfully, though, thinks people are a disposable part of the economy. When they prove too expensive, you can get rid of them. They'll find work somewhere. If they don't, they're losers.

First abolish the customer, say the economic fundamentalists, the EFs, and the tariffs that keep him in work, and move his job overseas to slave cultures, and all will be well.

It is the author's contention that this is wrong.

285

For a long time in my home state New South Wales there was a way of doing things known as Workfare.

The New South Wales government would give a job

like File Clerk Grade Three in the Water Board to a man who might otherwise not have a job at all.

He would go to the office Monday to Friday nine to five. He would do very little there. He would make little chains of paperclips. He would chat with other clerks by the water cooler. He would occasionally write a report on a subject of no great interest that would go into a file somewhere, unread. He would endure long hours of boredom.

In many ways his life was dispiriting.

But . . . he earned a wage, and married a wife, and bought a house and raised children and took them to Bondi Beach and walked with helium balloons along the cliffs above the sea and partook, in these and other ways, of the common life of humanity.

And he bought food, and tooth-braces, and school books, and shoes of varying sizes as his children grew, and helped keep the economy going.

Even though he produced no tangible goods at all.

286

And it's the only way an economy can be kept going.

By not making, or allegedly making, the manufacture and sale of goods its primary purpose, but the supply of money to humans, who then spend it on things, which in turn are manufactured by other humans who are also supplied with money and buy things.

Inasmuch as a Catholic priest was paid for an insubstantial product, so too was the file clerk, and so too, in many cases, is a professor of Assyrian studies or a CEO of a security company guarding world leaders from unseen, imagined assassins.

Inasmuch as a CEO is seen, though doing nothing, to be doing useful work, so too can anyone.

What sort of work might that be?

287

Well, there are several options.

They should include, as a priority, work that is good for self-esteem that can be done in country towns, since country towns are the crucial ingredient of a civilisation.

Without them a nation's population would be one vast teeming Manila, one vast filthy Mexico City, one vast noisome Calcutta. Or four or five of these diseased and squalid conurbations.

288

If the government built, or bought, in each big country town a theatre complex, which rented out theatrical spaces for twenty dollars a performance, that would help.

Small theatre groups would spontaneously form, and put on shows, and charge at the door not seventy dollars but ten or twelve, and the local cultural pride would improve.

If, furthermore, the government gave a wage of two hundred and fifty dollars a week to two hundred people – theatre directors, acting teachers, choreographers, designers, young actors, playwrights – selected by merit from the immediate locality, who then conceived and put on shows and toured them to other towns and earned their share of the ticket money at the door, a great deal of benefit to that country town would follow.

There would be less teenage crime, street violence, drug-taking, divorce, wife-beating, there would be more local pride and less emigration in despair to the fringes of big, pestiferous capital cities.

There would be no downside to it.

Except, of course, the eight million dollars the theatre complex would cost and the young participants' 2.6 million in annual wages.

Which isn't that much. It could be paid, each year, by the earnings of six poker machines in a local club, and a levy of three percent on the bookies at the local race track.

And the cost of the theatre could be paid by the government, much as it pays sixty billion or so for a fighter bomber.

Which is never used in battle, and never will be.

289

Should I say it now, or later?

Say it now, I think.

There is no such thing as economics, there is only *arithmetic*.

The more people have good jobs on good wages, the more they spend.

The more people that live good, long lives, the more they spend.

290

This art-led recovery plan could vary according to the town.

In one town it could be a concert hall and a symphony orchestra that are so subsidised. In another an opera house, and an opera company. In another an art school and an art gallery, with subsidised art teachers and promising art pupils. In another a puppetry and animation school, for the next generation of special effects. In another a college of modern music. In another an academy of boot-making, hat-making and costume design. In another an academy of French cooking or harpsichord playing, or country-and-western singing, or performance poetry.

In each building, or near it, studio flats should be available cheaply for those young people who are chosen, on merit, to work there.

Is there anything wrong with this?

291

It doesn't seem so.

It worked in Stratford, Ontario, where Shakespeare is put on year round and has been for fifty-six years. And in Niagara Falls where a George Bernard Shaw Festival keeps attracting tourists bored witless by adjacent cascading water. And Glyndebourne, and Galway and Hay-on-Wye and Adelaide, where various festivals attract people from across the world.

And it almost doesn't matter if no-one comes at all.

Because that many young people get work, and feel fulfilled, and spend money, and don't kill themselves in car accidents or go to gaol.

292

One young person killed at eighteen in a car accident costs the economy, in wages not earned and food not eaten and goods not bought, in the subsequent lifetime he never had, two and a half million dollars or thereabouts; discuss.

This is about a third of the cost of building the new local theatre.

One thousand such young people who might be saved by that theatre, or that gallery, or that concert hall, will by their early death cost the nation's economy five billion dollars; or thereabouts; discuss.

This sum would keep sixty-six small theatre companies going for a thousand years on the interest alone.

There is no such thing as economics, there is only arithmetic.

Discuss.

293

What I here suggest is not much different from what West Germany used to do, which was to subsidise in each major town a theatre group and a symphony orchestra and build places to put them in.

Nor is it all that different from an American religion which builds a big glass temple in a regional city and, by a combination of tithe, tax advantage and church collection plate, rings up a tidy profit and exalts the spirits of its proliferating congregation *though its product is entirely illusory* and boosts thereby the flagging economy of the region.

It doesn't matter what you pay them *for*. It only matters that you pay them.

294

You could give them a day's pay a week for learning and teaching Latin; for watching birds and writing about it; for asking old people about their lives and recording their memories; for studying (as F. D. Roosevelt paid John Steinbeck to do in the 1930s) the migratory patterns of certain infectious insects; for learning to play the harpsichord, or the one-stringed Japanese instrument the ichigenkin; for designing and building puppets that are then donated to primary schools; for taking people on eco-tours in public forests near the town; for teaching high-school kids to scuba dive; or juggle; or play the mouth organ; or sky-dive; or life-save; or compete at Olympic level in Grecian wrestling.

None of these things is an entirely worthless activity. All stimulate the community in some way and, if paid for, contribute to the economy.

And you never know what will be the most helpful in the end. It was Persian scholars who cracked the Enigma Code and did much to win World War II; discuss.

Nor is it much different from the many, many towns in America where various parts of superweapons are manufactured for use in coming wars that will never take place. The towns' economies are stimulated, food is bought, children raised, values affirmed, grandparenthood achieved, a measure of happiness enjoyed. And big, big rockets made.

And then junked.

All in the pursuit of a miasma, a hideous dream of worldwide nuclear war.

A delusion.

295

It doesn't matter what you pay them for. It only matters that you pay them.

Discuss.

296

Some people say that nobody will come to a local theatre staffed and run by local young people, but this is not so. Their parents and friends will come, for a start, just as they come to school plays and the town-hall performances of local brass bands and to local football games. Local is everything; local makes money.

And in this, as in all other things, it doesn't matter (yawn) what you pay them for. It only matters that you pay them.

A delusion makes money too.

297

But what do you pay them *with*?

Aye, there's the rub.

298

Icelandic króna are no good. Zimbabwe dollars vary astronomically. There is no call lately for Southern Confederate bonds or Roman sesterces. The chocolate that was currency in Peru is in abeyance.

The Australian dollar, moreover, has been lately aberrant, sometimes worth ninety-five US cents, sometimes fifty-one.

And, as we have seen, there are tremendous local advantages – in Bali, in Eritrea – in a local unexportable currency that tourist dollars for small things – carvings, paintings, tapa cloth – turn into local wealth.

So what should happen, probably, is this.

299

Pick the proportion to suit local needs, but a Third World employee should probably, by government decree and UN agreement, get ninety percent of his wage in local currency and ten percent in euros.

The local currency will pay for his food, rent and clothing and the euros for overseas travel, luxury goods and AIDS drugs and other medical supplies, if needed.

There should be restrictions, as there were in Gorbachev's Russia, on where the euros can be spent: special government-managed department stores where perfumes, cheeses, fine wines and thigh-length leather boots can be purchased with saved-up euros, and DVD players, and video games, and so on.

There will be difficulties with this, of course. There will be forged euros and barter and drug dollars and the prostitution of housewives, and so on, as there was in Russia. There will be problems getting euros not dollars in loans to central banks through the IMF and the World Bank, but the dollar, as we have seen by the trillions wasted by AIG, cannot be trusted.

There will be bribes and government corruption.

But it is likely the number of infants dying of bad water will come down, as more and more usable money is earned by farmers, builders, buskers, whores, hairdressers and bar staff, and spent on the necessities.

One of these dead infants, and fifteen have died while you were reading this chapter, could have been a Barack Obama, another a Miriam Makeba, another a Paul Robeson, another a Tiger Woods, and the money their talents might have added to the world economy is incalculable; discuss.

There go another three lost infants; I wonder what they were like, and what they could have done?

300

A few more things to consider about the Third World, sorry, the Developing World.

There should be a vast extension of the 'micro-economics' lending policy that has earned such dividends in the Subcontinent and a Nobel Prize for its inventor, Muhammad Yunus.

By this scheme peasant women are given loans of sometimes seventy dollars, sometimes a hundred, to set up a small business – the otherwise unaffordable price of a sewing machine, a loom, a milch-cow, a potter's wheel – with no security. No loans, or not very many, have been defaulted (in contrast with Freddie Mac and Fannie Mae and Lehman Brothers), and the ongoing, energising marketplace effect of industry, pride and the 'audacity of hope' has encouraged many, many Third

World people out of the despondent mire of their former existences into the beginnings of local, ebullient, small-town prosperity.

It will keep some workers in the small towns and stop them going to the grimy city fringes, into drugs and prostitution.

If the small towns, and the bigger towns, and the smaller cities can be made to survive, all will be well.

301

We have to see things as they truly are.

It's not money that matters – money is just a mood the nation is in, or the town is in – it's the purchasing power of the individual.

It's how you price things, and how often you buy them.

And how many of you there are.

302

You might call it Customer Economics (CE). Or more accurately Customer Arithmetic Economics (CAE).

The more customers there are, the better.

And there is no such thing as economics, there is only arithmetic.

303

Which means, and it's not rocket science (a halfwit can see it though not an academic economist), that eleven million dollars is better spent in a year by five hundred people than by one person.

By Jeff Skilling, for instance. Or Rodney Adler. Or John Elliott. Or Conrad Black. Or Alan Moss. Or Tom Cruise.

Five hundred people will buy more soap and soup and spanners and toothpaste and elective surgery than he will, and therefore multiply the purchase of other things.

It's not rocket science, it's arithmetic, simple arithmetic.

It's wrong that one man should get eleven million dollars in a year, and another man a hundred dollars in that year.

It's not rocket science, it's humanist morality.

It's justice.

Or something like justice.

Haven't seen it around for a while.

304

A simple act of parliament could fix this up at no great public cost: a law that says that no-one can get in wages or share-benefits any more than four times what the US President gets all up in a single year.

Not too hard to grasp, old friend. And not very hard to enact.

The argument that this will drive the most talented CEOs overseas will then arise, and there might be something in it.

And the answer is, 'Well then, let the greedy bastards

go. There'll be a bright young twenty-five-year-old pre-pared to work for as little as 1.5 million a year. You wait and see.'

The argument isn't really convincing anyway, I think. It's like Barack Obama saying, 'Unless you pay me five hundred million dollars a year if I win, I'm not running for President.'

And therefore saying we've lost *much more talented people than Barack Obama* to the private sector because the President, in any year, earns one six-hundred-and-eighty-eighth of what Oprah Winfrey earns.

Barack Obama is just the tip of the iceberg.

There are *really* bright guys out there, if only we had the money to pay for them.

Forget this Barack Obama.

He's a loser.

Otherwise he wouldn't be running.

His wages are just so low.

305

We should look at money carefully.

Money is just a mood the nation is in at a particular time.

One year it can pay ten million dollars for an Andy Warhol print; another year one hundred and fifty thou-sand dollars for a George Bush lecture; twenty million dollars for a panda; or a dollar for a house in Michigan.

Or eight trillion dollars for five loaves of bread in Zimbabwe.

Money can't be trusted. It can't be the ultimate measure of things.

What is the ultimate measure of things, you might ask?

A customer's need, I think, for what he can't do without.

A roof, for instance.

306

We have seen how the price of a house can be a dollar, or eight and a half thousand dollars, or 3.5 million dollars, and how this is ridiculous, and it has to be made less ridiculous.

What do we do about it?

307

Now this is hard.

It's very hard.

Most of the personal fortune of the middle class in most of the western world resides in the value, presumed or actual, of the house or the flat they live in. And if they think it's worth a million dollars, how are we to tell them it's in fact two hundred and fifty thousand dollars, and when they sell it, they should bring the price down?

And will they vote us out of government if they think we're being unfair?

You bet they will.

308

So I think the way to do it is this.

You pass a law that says no house with a lawn can be rented out for more than five hundred and twenty dollars a week, and no house without a lawn for more than four hundred dollars a week, and no penthouse apartment for more than three hundred and fifty dollars a week, and no flat for more than two hundred and eighty dollars a week.

If enforced, and you'll need a bureaucracy like the FBI to enforce it (but what else are they doing these days?), it will unleash an extra eighty-one billion dollars into the Australian economy, and one trillion one hundred million (or thereabouts) into the US economy, and three hundred billion (or thereabouts) into the British economy.

It will also force the price of houses down, over time, by about a half.

It will mean a lot of landlords will take a hit, but they can go to buggery. They can seek their profit margin in another sector of the economy. It will mean a lot of retirees will not have the income they planned on in their seventies. But they won't be like the AIG shareholders, or the Lehman Brothers shareholders, who lost everything. They'll have half the income they planned on, and have it for certain.

The purchasing power of the individual, however, will be increased; and, in the case of property owners, not diminished. They can buy another house, a house of equal value, with the price they get for the one they're currently in.

And all around them will be more available money, moving and working and changing hands, the way money does.

It won't be so bad when it all shakes down.

(Prove that I lie.)

And the extra, say, hundred dollars each flat-dweller will have when the rents come down will do the nation, and the national interest, a power of good.

Many will decide, because of the extra money, and the lower house prices, to have children after all.

Which means the economy will burgeon, and many, many more people become involved in its workings, and more taxpayers will be born, and work, and buy things.

Is there anyone out there with a better idea?

Speak up.

Or is there no alternative? No alternative to a million-dollar hovel you pay twelve hundred dollars a week for?

Funny you should ask.

309

There's this one.

You pass a law in parliament saying that after June 30th of the current calendar year any mortgage-holder *if he so wishes* can take up the following option *if he so wishes* of down-sizing his debt by half.

If, say, he (or she) has a mortgage of eight hundred thousand dollars costing him (or her) a thousand and seventy-six dollars in interest payments and principal per week, he (or she) can make that a *four*-hundred-thousand-dollar debt by yielding up half the *ownership* of the property to the bank.

The mortgagor stays in the house as long as he or she likes. When the property is finally sold, at a time convenient to the mortgagor, the bank gets half the takings.

This gives the mortgagor five hundred dollars more a week to spend. And the bank has more equity in property to borrow money with.

This would add a hundred and four billion more per year to the Australian economy, three hundred and seventy billion to the British economy and 1.5 trillion to the American economy.

It might annoy some bank CEOs, who might have to post a profit not of four billion but two billion some years, but tough on them.

The benefits to the *economy*, and to the emotional health of the householders, and the happiness of their marriage, and their willingness to have more children, would be enormous.

310

You could add to that a second option.

The eight–hundred-thousand-dollar property debt could be exchanged for a thirty-year *leasehold* costing two hundred and eighty thousand dollars.

This would give the bank even more equity to borrow on, and give middle-aged childless couples, or elderly couples, or young couples starting out, seven hundred dollars more to spend each week.

311

If there is a quarrel against these two scenarios, and the knock-on buckets of money they would add to each community and each nation that took them up, I need to hear it.

The only one that comes to mind is that *banks should have it easy while the people suffer. This has been forever the divine right of kings, and it shouldn't change now.*

312

This massive boost to the economy and the national happiness could be achieved by a single act of parliament that only seven percent of the public would oppose, some bank executives, academic economists and the miserable craven underlings of Rupert Murdoch.

Because those who don't want to halve their debt wouldn't have to. They could run their lives as they originally planned.

And the bank CEOs thus shamed could get out of the banking business if they chose, and seek work in some other sector of the economy.

There would be plenty of greedy young bastards to

take their place, who would work with the New Mortgage Order (NMO) with guile and cunning.

313

'The workings of the market' is another way of saying, it seems, 'God moves in mysterious ways'.

Discuss.

314

While writing the present chapter the author became aware of swine flu, soon to be a pandemic some say, and noted its resemblance to global finance.

It goes everywhere, like the wind. It knocks down humans in a rapid progression, like a falling row of dominoes. It resists regulation. It kills children first, and then young adults, at the start of their working lives. It cares not whom it kills.

It can be resisted by what one might call, without hesitation, 'protection': by face-masks, hand-washing, avoiding doctors' waiting rooms and stopping those who might carry the virus crossing the border.

One resists it as one might resist a multinational corporation.

And for the same reason, that it ruins lives.

Tens of thousands, millions of lives.

One protects oneself from it.

What a good idea that is.

FROM EACH ACCORDING
TO HIS

315

There are a good few things more to mention, and more the author will think of, I guess, long after this book is published.

One involves a particular thought on the theft of time.

I quote a typical conversation I had this morning with a plausible male voice in the telephone exchange.

'Welcome to Telstra Directory Assistance. Your call may be monitored and recorded for quality purposes. What name please?'

'Canberra Cabs.'

'What town or suburb?'

'Canberra.'

'I'm sorry, could you tell me what town or suburb.'

'Canberra, ACT.'

'Let me look that up.' (Long pause.) 'I found four departments or sub-listings. One for CityRail timetables for feedback service for metropolitan and outer metropolitan areas; one for CountryLink rail and coach information; one for interstate enquiries and one for

RailCorp Corruption Prevention Line. Which one do you want?'

'I want none of those.'

'I hear . . . CityRail timetable feedback service for metropolitan and outer metropolitan areas in . . . Canberra. Right?'

'No.'

'Please hold for an operator.'

In another ten seconds I had the number for, as it turned out, Canberra Taxis Combined. It answered promptly, and another pleasing male voice said:

'Thank you for calling Taxis Combined. Your call will be answered by the first available operator and may be recorded for quality purposes. You may wish to book your next cab at Taxis Combined dot com dot a-u. For now, please hold the line.'

Seven seconds of not unpleasing music followed, after which an elocuted female voice revealed, 'You're talking to a computer speech recognition system. To book a taxi, say "yes"; to check a booking say "check"; for anything else say "no".'

'Yes.'

'What suburb are we picking you up from?'

'Parliament House.'

'What house number and street are we picking you up from?'

'I don't know. It's Parliament House.'

'Sorry, what house number and street are we picking you up from?'

'I don't know. It's Parliament House. The House of Representatives entrance, it's a well-known landmark.'

'Please wait a moment while I transfer you to an operator.'

Five more seconds of, again, quite pleasing music, and then, at last, a sensate human.

'Taxis Combined. Eileen speaking. Are you making or checking a booking please?'

'Your computer doesn't know where Parliament House is. Could you please . . . teach it?'

'Wait a minute, I'll look it up on the map . . . Oh, there it is!' She was being ironic I'm sure.

The two minutes forty-eight seconds all this took cost me one dollar twenty. Many, many elected parliamentarians have suffered the last half of it in the last eight months, at a cost to their health and blood pressure and the common weal that cannot easily be calculated. One of them imitates a moron and gets through to an operator immediately. I predict he will be Prime Minister.

The net cost to the nation per year of this theft of time and happiness is hard to assess. To the people of Canberra it would be (and this is my estimate) six hundred and fifty-seven thousand dollars a year, or a dollar twenty-five a minute.

316

All of this occurs to save the company perhaps twelve hundred dollars a week, an amount two taxi drivers can earn in three shifts, the sum which would employ three more people on earphones round the clock. It happens so as to give the twelve hundred dollars to the CEO, Mark Bramston, on top of the twenty-six thousand or thereabouts (correct me if I'm wrong) he gets each week. There is no other reason for it than this.

Four hundred man-hours I would guess are wasted in Canberra a day by this depleting cross-purposes humiliation, and it should be outlawed. For it echoes what happens when you ring a theatre, a newspaper, a weather bureau, a cinema complex.

You suffer a theft of your time, a pilfering of the life you have on earth. If like me you are sixty-seven it gets to you.

At the Sydney Theatre Company, however, a state-subsidised concern run by Cate Blanchett and her husband, you always get through to a human who puts you through to another human, who immediately understands your needs. This gratifies you and makes you want to go to that theatre a lot.

I propose a new law, therefore, that requires every company that employs more than twenty people to employ two telephonists, who may also double as receptionists and typists, and every company that employs more than a hundred people four telephonists, and so on.

And in these companies there shall be no recorded voices whatever.

And the money shall come out of the vast wage formerly paid to the CEO.

This law would increase teenage employment, give the young people concerned an understanding of the company they work for, which may lead to promotion within it, and save the nation and therefore the economy tens of millions of wasted man-hours, wasted thinking time, wasted earning time, in a year.

317

While writing this chapter the author went by taxi from his office in the CBD to his dentist in Gordon, in Sydney's northern suburbs.

There were ill-timed red traffic lights all the way, and five thousand cars crawling at an infant's pace for ten weary miles, and a journey normally twenty minutes took fifty-two.

While the author was gum-injected, scraped and drilled and flat on his back on the tilting chair watching *Death at a Funeral* on the ceiling television, he pondered the time thieved from the lives of its victims by that one traffic jam (two thousand six hundred and sixty-six man-hours) because of the traffic lights' incompetence, and the cost of this to the nation's economy of those lost thirty-two minutes (sixty-four thousand dollars, probably).

He then, while the drill went in, pondered what it would cost (one hundred and thirty dollars) for five traffic cops for the hour that would have sorted it out, reducing the loss of time, happiness and (probably) money by half.

He then multiplied that traffic jam by the five that happen on similar roads every day, and what that would (notionally) cost the nation (allowing for those who were not driving to or from work), which is three hundred and twenty thousand dollars for that day alone.

As opposed to the cost of twenty-five traffic cops for that day, which is six hundred and fifty dollars.

With the contrasting cost per year of people not machines, nine hundred and twelve thousand dollars not seven hundred and thirty-two dollars – or thereabouts – he wondered why, *against all mathematics*, the relevant bureaucrats preferred the much more expensive machines, whose incompetence was now proved, to the much cheaper humans who, on these five roads anyway, could better do the job.

He decided that the answer must be that bureaucrats, these days, bureaucrats who feel they must ape the efficiencies of the private sector whatever they do, were in the *habit* of not even thinking about it, but hiring machines instead of humans willy-nilly, because this is what you did. This is what corporations do, and what bureaucrats do now in every branch of government.

The way they do on buses. Every bus on earth, for the

reasons stated above, should have a young male conductor, instead of a juggernaut of vigilant television cameras and automated ticket machines. For among other things this gives the young man employment, the habit of work, the pleasure of social contact. It also speeds up the journey, protects young female passengers from harassment and fear, and saves hundreds of millions of hours from the theft of time.

318

I noticed this morning, May Day 2009, another theft of time, when ringing a friend's mobile phone. It was switched off, and after five rings, taking thirteen seconds, there was a *pause* of three seconds before he spoke his message.

This pause, connived by the greedy, scarpering Sol Trujillo (one hundred and twenty-nine dollars a minute, waking or sleeping, for the rest of his life, on the interest on his payout alone), will cost Australian phone users, in my rough estimate, five hundred and twenty-one million dollars this year, 2009, a year when we could use the money.

319

I also realised, a few hours later, that his rival Vodafone was making even more money when I rang 121 for my messages. 'Hi there, voicemail has space for only . . . four messages. Please delete any unwanted messages. You have . . . two new messages, and . . . sixteen saved messages. First message received . . . Monday . . . May . . . the fourth at . . . nine . . . fourteen . . . a.m.', and so on. This took sixty-three seconds, cost me a dollar fifty-six cents (since Vodafone has a sixty-second billing system for prepaid customers in which you're charged seventy-eight cents for each call within one minute and another seventy-eight cents for any second over a minute) and Australia's phone users, at my estimate, one hundred and seven million dollars in a year.

320

There could be, I suppose, a law that assesses and punishes Crimes Against The Economy (CATE), like other laws that assess and punish crimes against humanity, with a penalty of three years in gaol, which was what Alan Bond got for stealing a billion dollars. These would include Sol's phone pause, and Dick Fuld's bonus, and Oprah Winfrey's two hundred and seventy-five million dollars in a year, and Ken Lay's two-hundred-and-fifty-million-dollar annual wage, money that seems unearned, like a bank robber's takings, or the millions in ransom a Somalian pirate gets from kidnapping passengers.

Crimes Against The Economy.

You know it makes sense.

It could include those CEOs who refuse to pass on the

Reserve Bank's lowered interest rates, and pay themselves, like Mike Smith at the ANZ, 12.96 million dollars a year.

Three years in gaol is not so bad.

It's what a teenager might get for stealing his fifth television to pay for drugs.

321

There should also be a law declaring a new crime, Industrial Manslaughter, which, after an avoidable accident that kills people, puts on trial the CEO of a company, who if found guilty goes away for six and a half years, the average sentence for ordinary manslaughter.

Which would bring down the number of youth deaths, and expand the economy – sorry, the arithmetic – some more.

WHO/WHOM, AS THE GREAT MAN SAID

322

In the last thirty years, the questions, the answers and the basic argument have been the same. The argument always comes back to teenagers and whether they are by the age of nineteen in the habit of work.

If they aren't – and they feel their lives are futile and they're drawn into drugs and prostitution, or member-ship in a bikie gang or a chiliastic religion, or their souls are wasted in these or other ways – it's a pity, and it's worth preventing.

How do we do this?

323

A form of Pacifistic National Service (PNS) might be a good idea.

And it might cost no more than a couple of Star Wars rockets we no longer need, and could cancel now. Or, in Australia, two useless nuclear submarines that won't be delivered till 2015 when they'll be out of date.

The idea would be some variant on this.

For six months of a young person's nineteenth year, on a wage of three hundred and twenty dollars a week, with hostel accommodation provided, he or she could clear trails through eco-tour forests, or replant vegetation after bushfires, or teach little children to swim, or look after old women, making their beds and bringing their food and listening to them reminisce, or help look after young mothers immediately after childbirth (as the French do) . . .

. . . and in *return* for this, they get three years of university, studying whatever they want, or a plumber's apprenticeship, or a nurse's degree, or the price of a pick-up truck and a circular saw to start their own small business with, or whatever.

And if they choose to do a six-year medical degree, they must oblige themselves to be for two years after graduation a GP in a remote country town.

This, if done, would get them into the *habit of work* and some plan in their life that might get them through it.

Especially if the tariffs come back, and the jobs therefore to their towns.

It would also help old people, in their declining, distressed and lonely years, to have someone young to talk to and share the past with.

And it would cost less, and be more useful and rewarding, than sending them to Iraq. Or Afghanistan.

324

Am I asking too much here?

Wouldn't it be better, really, wouldn't it be truly better, old friend, to let the market choose who lives and who dies, and who endures existences of regret and misery, and not regulate, or try to regulate, the amount of misery, loss and desperation there is?

To let the market choose who loses and who wins, without government interference?

To let the next Einstein, Obama, McCartney, Hawking, Roosevelt slip through the cracks?

I mean, if he's a loser, he'll be a loser whatever the hell you do for him.

Better to get rid of him, as Hitler did mental defectives.

Saves thinking, saves worry.

325

There are some other things, almost too obvious to mention.

Pass a law that declares all cars more than seven years old illegal. Require their owners to junk them and buy in their place a green car the government approves, or travel by train.

Double the number of trains now available. Put dining cars on them that commuters can have breakfast in on the way to work. Solar-power them. This will take a lot of cars off the road and reduce global warming.

Bring back the Hindenburg. It's safe, stable, clean energy. It crosses the Atlantic as fast as the *Queen Mary 2*. It's luxurious, uplifting, self-affirming. Give it, like Blackwater, another name.

Cut by half the number of jumbo jets. They cause, at that altitude, more global warming than any other vehicle. Encourage people to take the Hindenburg.

Power as many countries as you can with 'hot rocks'. You pour water down a hole, which comes back spurting up as steam, which powers things. The steam then condenses into water, which you pour back down the hole. Adelaide could be powered on the hot rocks currently available in South Australia. There will be more hot rocks in New Zealand, Yellowstone Park, the Andes, Krakatoa, Stromboli, and so on.

Put a good deal of the Australian, New Mexican and Chilean deserts under glass and solar-power electricity into batteries which then sell worldwide.

Keep mining and burning coal, but pipe the smoke into ponds with special forms of oil-rich micro-algae that eat the CO2. This algae then dies and is compressed into bricks, yielding up an oil that fuels in turn, along with coal, the power station.

Grow marijuana in vast plantations, the non-hallucinogenic sort that matures in three months, and out of it manufacture cloth, paper, chopsticks, hats and furniture in factories in country towns employing scores of young people. It grows four times as fast as its competition, plantation wood, and uses much less water than its competition cotton. The 'reefer madness' campaign that saw it banned in the early twentieth century was in part got up by the cotton industry, a low-paid or slave-wage racket, and it worked.

Buy up each year the entire opium-poppy crop of Afghanistan and give it gratis to the hospices of the Third World, which are probably in need of it. This would save the lives of a lot of western junkies, prop up the family incomes of a lot of Afghan farmers, lessen the income of the Taliban and the scum they buy weapons from, and save the lives of a lot of soldiers otherwise obliged to go in with flame-throwers annoying the local population. It would also reduce by tens of billions the annual Black Economy of the western world, the which abundant money could fund more helpful things than drugged oblivion. Pay for all this with an annual ten dollar tax on the householders of the western world.

Give no male child a driver's licence till he is twenty-four, when his brain is fully formed, and he becomes aware he is not immortal and speed kills, and let girls, who drive more safely, do so at eighteen. This will save many lives, reduce parental trauma and add with lengthened lives and emptier hospitals to the world's economy five hundred billion dollars at least (my estimate) in the next fifty years.

Add to the American economy a GST, a tax on things sold, of eight percent. Increase the GST in Australia from ten to twelve percent, and make a similar increase in Britain. This invisible slug, which rises as prices rise, will in three years pay back the vast deficits each western country is currently suffering because of the Meltdown. When the deficits are paid off, put the GST down again to its former level.

Pass a law requiring all ceilings in houses henceforth to be at least nine feet above the floor. This will reduce depression, suicide, serial killing, argumentative marriage and poor exam results and increase the earnings of bricklayers. If you don't believe high ceilings increase happiness go to any town hall or any nineteenth-century church, assess how you feel and then go home.

Give every child who graduates from high school a laptop computer (this already happens in parts of Australia) and a digital movie camera. Give every schoolteacher of twenty years' experience a specially struck gold medal. Subsidise the ownership in old age of dogs who are sympathetic listeners and good role models.

To pay for this, cut by half all expenditure on war weapons and presidential security and impose a tax of thirty percent on all religions. This would raise, in the United States, in excess of two trillion dollars each year. And, oh yes . . .

. . . bring down by two-thirds the number of economics

courses in universities, and outlaw all but the Keynes-leaning ones. All the others have been, as we have seen here, devastatingly harmful, and the cause of hundreds of millions of needless deaths, more than Nazism, Communism, Pol Pot and Rwanda put together. Bring to trial at The Hague Alan Greenspan, disciple of Ayn Rand, for crimes against humanity and give him, if not prison, a severe talking-to. Dig up Milton Friedman's bones and pelt them with dung. Treat his theories as you would Creationism, with unanimous contempt.

<h3 style="text-align:center">326</h3>

Acknowledge, furthermore, while you're up, that Gorbachev was a good thing for Russia, and Putin a bad thing. Under Gorbachev, everyone had a roof, a job, a wage as good as a kindergarten teacher in the West, the best public transport, the best theatre, ballet, public parks and circuses, opera and subsidised cinema in the world; plus too much alcoholism, abortion, divorce, part-time prostitution of housewives to western tourists, and so on. Putin runs a fascist corporate police state much like Mussolini's, full of criminal billionaires and beggars freezing to death in the streets and the routine assassination of journalists and rival politicians, like Lebed.

Make all medical treatment free and good, as it is in Cuba. Give every African who needs it AIDS treatment free. Work out a way, with solar power, to clean up Africa's water; it's not that hard. Boil the water, turn it into steam, condense it, pour it in a cup and drink it. Make simple machines that do this available in every village.

Remember every child that dies costs the world economy in goods not bought, and taxes not paid, an average of one million seven hundred and twenty-eight thousand dollars; or, if he or she is an African, one-tenth of that.

327

While writing the last chapter the author saw on the television news an Air France plane had vanished in a big turbulent storm and two hundred and forty-nine people, probably, were killed when it broke up and fell in flames into the Atlantic.

To answer the obvious question of what the fuck the plane and its pilot were doing in a big turbulent storm over the Atlantic in the first place, you must realise that airline policy, and the airline's profit, forbade him to fly around it. Each plane gets only enough petrol to get there, flying straight. If the pilot takes a big detour he falls short, in the sea. So he flies straight, picking his way through the storm, knowing he will be struck by lightning and hoping this doesn't do too much damage.

And the CEO saves, oh, a hundred, two hundred thousand dollars a year which he keeps for himself, by buying less petrol for a plane that therefore crashes in the sea.

You know it makes sense.

There is no alternative.

328

The last question to answer, and it's not a hard one, old friend, is how much the government should do, and how much the 'private sector' (that is, jackal capitalism) should be trusted to do now we've seen it's full of greedy, conscienceless bastards so self-absorbed they've lately killed four hundred thousand *more* children (according to Gordon Brown, who is good at figures) and laid waste the system they grew rich on.

329

It's not too hard to answer this question of who/whom, who benefits, because there's a lot of evidence before us, of what works and what doesn't.

Socialised restaurants, Cuba has proved, are bloody awful, the waiters haughty, the dishes dirty, the food inedible.

So restaurants should probably always be in the 'private sector'.

Private medicine, and private insurance for medical care, however, kill between them hundreds of millions of people prematurely, Barack Obama's mother among them.

So the medical business, all of it, including the

manufacture of drugs, should be run by governments. They can break the whole thing up into departments, cancer, diabetes, pregnancy, whatever, and the various government departments can compete for lottery earnings and government windfalls, but no private institution should be let anywhere near it. They kill too many people.

Far, far too many people.

The US medical system lost the American economy around twenty-two billion in cash unspent last year because it wasn't the *Canadian* medical system, in which people live longer. The private medicos kill too many people. Many more than Somalian pirates, or, as I like to call them, privateers. Twenty-two billion is a lot of money.

There seems no argument, however, against chemists' shops being privately run. Or fruiterers. Or corner groceries. Or tailors. Or shoe shops, watchmakers, key-cutters, dry-cleaners, chiropractors, tango schools, gymnasiums, hairdressers, pie shops, masseurs and so on.

Telephone services should be socialised, as we have argued above. And all phone calls to anywhere on earth should be five cents for three minutes and ten cents an hour.

Why should they not be?

330

There seems no argument, once you look at the BBC, Mosfilm, the Polish, French, Hungarian, Czech, Icelandic and Irish film industries, the Royal Shakespeare Company, the National Theatre of Scotland, the Rustaveli Theatre, the Bolshoi Ballet and so on, that the entertainment industry should not be socialised, or largely socialised. A fair model is the French film industry which is funded, or funded largely, by a 10.7 percent levy on all cinema tickets and subsidises thereby through bureaucratic committees the most consistently good cinema in the history of the world.

Different countries have different tastes of course. Some, like Poland, want more money for puppetry. Some, like the South Americans, favour films about cannibalism. Some, like Scotland, favour plays with very bad language. This can be sorted out by bureaucrats and committees and boards of directors in differing competing entities, BBC1 versus BBC2 versus Channel 4 versus RSC versus the National versus Glyndebourne Opera, or whatever.

But the socialist model is clearly superior, and attracts many tourists, and should be therefore funded mightily. In any contest between unsubsidised, exuberant, money-grubbing, non-risk-taking Broadway and the Royal National Theatre, or the Scottish National Theatre, the British model comes out on top every time. As does BBC News versus Fox News. Or Richard Dimbleby versus Glenn Beck.

Or am I wrong about this?

331

We should close down SDI, Star Wars, of course, Reagan's faster-than-a-speeding-bullet nonsense, and halve the Pentagon budget, thus saving about three hundred and seventy-five billion dollars a year, and use the armaments factories in every American state to build green cars, solar panels, Hindenburgs, safe new ferries and fast trains powered by wind or sunlight. And . . .

332

Is there anything else?

We have seen that global capitalists are a pack of marauding bastards who don't care who they kill or ruin and who don't deserve the trillions they pay themselves for making carcinogens and cluster-bombs and hedge funds that blow up the world's economy, and . . .

Oh yes.

How do we stop them?

333

Drawing out of a hat the name of one every three months and putting him or her in gaol for six months wouldn't hurt. But I doubt Obama, who wants to 'save capitalism from itself' for some reason, would be in this.

We can do something quite sensible, however.

We can pass a couple of laws.

334

One says that any global corporation digging for coal, oil, bauxite, aluminium, uranium or whatever must spend two-thirds of the money it makes in the country it is gouging.

And it must work in a fifty-fifty partnership with the government of that country. And that country, by a UN mandate, cannot vary this agreement, ever.

And half of that government's money goes into its health system.

335

And another law that says . . .

I'm not sure I should say this, it's so simple I might look like a fool. At this late stage, a fool.

But it works, I think.

336

Pass a law that limits the size of a corporation, along lines to be discussed.

A law that says, for instance, that Wal-Mart can only have three big stores in Minnesota and two in Arizona, in remote places, and you have to travel a long way to get to them.

This will mean the corporation will make less money, and will sell its goods at a higher price.

This will mean the corner grocery store can compete

with them, and will not go broke, or will not go broke for certain.

It will mean there are more small businesses, more economic activity, more prosperity, more purchasing power for individuals.

Imagine a law that said that McDonald's could have only five outlets in any city.

This would mean a hundred more small fast-food outlets, with proud greasy chefs competing in quality for better hamburgers, chicken burgers, coffee, french fries. Word of mouth would make sure the fittest survived.

And it might not be McDonald's.

337

And we should cut in half the government money spent on Security – what I call the Paranoia Industries (PI). It is mostly wasted as I proved when I entered four times the Australian Federal Parliament with a Swiss army knife and twice got within two feet of the then Prime Minister, John Howard, whom I dislike.

And as some young satirists proved when a man dressed as Osama bin Laden got within twenty yards of the Sydney headquarters of George W. Bush.

No-one significant has been killed (save Benazir Bhutto, who had no security at all, and Olof Palme, who had no security at all, and Anna Lindh, who had no security at all, and Yitzhak Rabin, who had very little security, and about twenty Muslim leaders who had no security at all) in twenty-five years.

So whatever the security precautions were in 1983, however many bodyguards and following helicopters it took then, should be the number it takes now.

About one-third of the current number, I would guess.

Which would save us a whole lot of money.

338

The fastest-growing industry on earth is the security industry.

And like a lot of capitalism, it offers as its outcome an intangible product, something that in the end *does not happen*.

And may never have happened at all.

And may never *happen* at all.

Like an Afterlife full of ten-gallon hats and Jerry Falwell's relatives and lions lying down with lambs.

Getting rid of half this superstition would save us a whole lot of money.

339

So would cutting all prison sentences to a maximum of five years.

If they haven't got the point by then, they never will. And little implanted radios stuck in their legs would let us know where they are, very cheaply.

And billions and billions of money devoted to human misery would be spent elsewhere.

340

And there's one more thing, I'm afraid.

This time round there is, anyway.

This is the banning of all advertising on television.

341

This would facilitate competition. A new product could compete *on a level playing field* with an old, established one – like, say, Coca-Cola.

It would mean that word of mouth, not propaganda, was why you bought things.

It would *localise* the things you bought. Like soft drinks, lollies, jeans, cosmetics, which would compete with global ones and, maybe, outdo them.

And the cost of the global things, relieved of the burden of what, a trillion a year? five hundred billion a year? in advertising costs, would come down by a quarter, or a half.

And living would be cheaper therefore.

342

There would still be advertising on radio and in local newspapers.

But the high-cost television product, on free-to-air, cable and the internet, would go.

And would television therefore implode and cease to be?

It hasn't in England in the seventy-seven years of BBC-TV. A licence fee of a hundred and forty-two pounds a year per TV set funds the BBC still. It's not that much to ask. It's one pound ten a week per person watching. It's not that much. It's a lot less than the thousands he (or she) pays to watch television ads.

And DVDs would be still available, of Hollywood movies past and present, and the golden age of TV comedy, and miniseries like *Rome, John Adams, Big Love, Mad Men,* the Jane Austen adaptations, the Shakespeare series, and so on.

What would be the problem?

Some advertising executives losing their five million a year?

Really?

Is that a problem?

343

Let us sum up now.

Capitalism has killed a lot of people and, by its own measurement, failed. It ran on rules and expectations that were, a good deal of the time, illusory. It marketed products that did not exist, and was noted a few times doing so. Many of its brightest stars went to gaol for pretending to a reality that was either non-existent or crazy. Others awarded themselves billions for failing and tiptoed out the door, with bags of jingling moolah in their overloaded arms.

Capitalism hired academics to back up its deluded propositions, bribed governments to buy products, like Star Wars rockets that would never work, plus atomic bombs that would never be used, plus cluster-bombs that should never have been used. It bombed flat whole countries and rebuilt them, to improve its bottom lines.

It killed, maimed, impoverished and drove into exile twenty-two million people, probably (I include the children killed by bad water and AIDS), in the last five years.

344

Social democracy, by contrast, has killed fewer people, probably twenty million fewer people, and saved and improved the lives of many more. In Sweden, Norway, Denmark, Holland, Austria, France, New Zealand, Ireland and Canada and, to a lesser extent, Venezuela and Australia, it has provided an agreeable system in difficult times with a fair deal of justice and good subsidised movies, to one hundred and eighty-five million people.

It has done so by regulation and nationalised industries, an inquisitive bureaucracy and *national standards* that have, in many places, the force of religion.

Social democracy has proved it is not an illusion. Though agnostic, and bureaucratic, and nit-picking, and complex in its many incarnations, it is merciful at its heart, where capitalism is cruel at its heart. And murderous. And greedy. And shameless. And very close to psychotic. And it kills, and cripples, and maddens, and sickens many, many more people than social democracy.

And people don't like it any more.

They're mad as hell, and they're not going to take it any more.

345

And they don't have to.

There *is* an alternative.

It is in these pages, and in many good countries, and in many decent human hearts across this planet.

Prove that I lie.